THE SPIRIT OF ADOPTION

RANDY & KELSEY BOHLENDER

The Spirit of Adoption: Winning the Battle for the Children
By Randy and Kelsey Bohlender

Published by The Zoe Foundation
PO Box #481772
Kansas City, MO 64148
www.thezoefoundation.com

ISBN: 978-0-9828919-0-2

Unless otherwise noted, all Scriptural quotations are from the New King James Version of the Bible. Copyright © 1979, 1980, 1982, by Thomas Nelson, Inc., publishers.

Scripture quotations marked NIV are taken from THE HOLY BIBLE, NEW INTERNATIONAL VERSION®, NIV® Copyright © 1973, 1978, 1984 by the International Bible Society. Used by permission of Zondervan. All rights reserved.

Scriptural quotations marked NLT are taken from the are taken from the Holy Bible, New Living Translation, copyright 1996, 2004. Used by permission of Tyndale House Publishers, Inc., Wheaton, Illinois 60189. All rights reserved.

Design by King+Sons Design
Back cover photography by Shelley Paulson Photography

Printed in the United States of America

To our seven arrows,
Jackson, Grayson, Zion, Zoe, Anna, Mercy and Piper.
We look at your lives and know that what we do is worth it.

To Derek Loux.
Your passion for the Lord and the orphan was contagious
and your vision lives on, dear friend.
You were a true revolutionary.

CONTENTS

Acknowledgements   vii

Foreword   1

1   The Spirit of Elijah   7

2   The New Underground Railroad   13

3   The Battle for the Children   25

4   The Great Finalization   37

5   Giving and Receiving Life   47

6   Divine Dreams   57

7   The Rewiring of the American Dream   69

8   Myths about Adoption   81

9   Generational Links   93

10   The Call to Action   105

11   The Charge   115

The Zoe Foundation   119

ACKNOWLEDGEMENTS

Lou and Therese Engle — *You have taught us how to dream with God and believe in the impossible. You imparted an unquenchable desire to be mothers and fathers to the next generation. Truly, you both are an example of the spirit of Elijah.*

The Zoe Foundation Team — *You guys rock! We love you all and consider it an honor to stand with you, shoulder to shoulder, fighting for life.*

Grandma Bohlender — *You continue to amaze us! Your willingness to endure the chaos surrounding seven children and two quirky adults is inspiring. We love you!*

JHOP — *We were indelibly marked in those months standing with you before the Supreme Court and continue to stand with you in the battle for righteousness and justice.*

Mike Bickle — *You have challenged our community to love the orphan without reservation. The rescued children will be a part of your eternal reward.*

Steve Sjogren — *We will never forget how you showed us that "small things done with great love will change the world". We aspire to demonstrate the spirit of generosity that you have displayed towards us.*

Katrina Styles, Christina Styles, Annie Peterson and Laura Goodwin — *We have adopted you into our family forever! You have sacrificially given of yourselves to us and our children. You make it possible for us to do what we do. We love you!*

John and Tracie Loux — *We so enjoy the melding of our lives and work with yours. You truly understand our brand of crazy, having clearly chosen it as your own as well. We get to do this!*

Foreword

R_{oe} v. *Wade*, that infamous court case that legalized abortion on-demand in America, took place on January 22, 1973. The date 1/22, I believe, is not without great significance. There was another decree of death issued on a 1/22. Exodus 1:22, "So Pharaoh commanded all his people, saying, 'Every son who is born you shall cast into the river...'"

The verses that follow—describing the birth, adoption, foster care, and training of Moses—unfold the biblical prescription for the overthrow and destruction of all the beastly death regimes throughout history. God simply brings forth a child that causes the death system to crumble. Deliverance is always found in a mother's womb or an adoptive mother's caring heart. Don't you love God's story? One adopted child shakes the Pharaohs and the Herods from their thrones.

God uses the weakness of the womb to pull down the power of the proud. Satan always seeks to destroy the child for the child is the sign of the imminent demise of the rebel regime. It is always, "For unto us a Child is born, unto us a Son is given, and the government will be upon His shoulders." (Isaiah 9:6)

The primordial prophecy of the ancient battle between the seed and the serpent is proclaimed in Genesis 3:15. The Lord speaks to the serpent, saying, "And I will put enmity between you and the woman, and between your seed and her Seed; He shall bruise your head and you shall bruise His heel."

That which began in a little garden in Eden is manifested in the end-time cosmic battle unfolded in Revelation 12:1-7.

"A great and wondrous sign appeared in heaven: a woman clothed with the sun, with the moon under her feet and a crown of twelve stars on her head. She was pregnant and cried out in pain as she was about to give birth. Then another sign appeared in heaven: an enormous red dragon with seven heads and ten horns and seven crowns on his heads. His tail swept a third of the stars out of the sky and flung them to the earth. The dragon stood in front of the woman who was about to give birth, so that he might devour her child the moment it was born. She gave birth to a son, a male child, who will rule all the nations with an iron scepter. And her child was snatched up to God and to his throne. The woman fled into the desert to a place prepared for her by God, where she might be taken care of for 1,260 days. And there was war in heaven. Michael and his angels fought against the dragon, and the dragon and his angels fought back."

The last days inaugurate a worldwide assault on the offspring of God. All the cosmic and angelic hosts are deployed in the heavenly war over the seed. This heavenly battle is now being manifested on the earth in a rage of terror against children. Since 1973, abortion has killed 50 million babies. If the scourge of abortion does not wipe out the seed, the onslaught of divorce further assaults the children.

God roars through the prophet Malachi, declaring, "I hate divorce." Why? Because, "I am seeking a godly offspring." If the rampage of divorce does not destroy the seed, there are further attacks in the way of child abuse, child pornography, child molestation, child slavery, and child soldiers. But, into this holocaust steps a new army of rescuers. They are the prophetic fulfillment of the great last days antidote for the breakdown of society.

"Behold, I will send you Elijah the prophet before the coming of the great and dreadful day of the LORD. And he will turn the hearts of the fathers to the children, and the hearts of the children to their fathers." (Malachi 4: 5, 6)

The most prophetic thing you can do in this present age is adopt a child. Twenty years ago, I had a dream in which orphans were crying out to me, "Don't just take care of your own children, take care of us!" Later, I dreamed of civilization crumbling to the ground, and I was out in the field rescuing babies who were barely surviving.

Sovereignly, the Lord called me into a community of families to take on the abortion issue and raise up a prayer movement to end *Roe* v. *Wade*. Our precious friends, Randy and Kelsey Bohlender were a part of that community. How God knit our hearts together in love. God began to respond to our prayers for the unborn and the pregnant mother. It was similar to when Jesus said, "Pray the Lord of the harvest, Send forth laborers into the harvest field." And then He sent those praying disciples into the harvest field as the answer to their own prayers. The disciples became the apostles, the sent ones.

The Spirit of the Lord began to stir us that it was not enough to pray for the ending of abortion. We needed to put feet to our prayers. I will never forget that historic moment in Fort Mill, South Carolina, in a large tent gathering with Jason Upton leading worship and causing our hearts to burn for the spirit of adoption under the love of the Father. Then Kelsey Bohlender stood and proclaimed a glorious vision that changed us for eternity. She heralded a vision of one million adoptions, punctuating the message with profound prophetic confirmation. Did not our hearts burn within us in that glorious tent of meeting? The hand of the Lord was coming on the Bohlender family.

This book that you are now reading tells the vision and the story. Together, we have been caught up into a movement. The Bohlenders' adoption story is off the charts. We are no longer just dreaming, but seeing children who would have been aborted and are now being adopted. Could this happen throughout the whole land? Yes! We believe!

Wherever I go I run into young women and families who want to adopt children. The last days spirit of adoption is being poured out because a Moses is rising. An anointed one is coming and the survivors will become the saviors of a generation.

Let this book be a clarion call, "Every child, a wanted child" and an enlistment paper for "friends of the family" and "friends of God" like Randy and Kelsey Bohlender. Let us be doers of the Word and not merely hearers. God, release the spirit of adoption.

Lou Engle
July 21, 2010

ONE

The Spirit of Elijah

"Behold, I will send you Elijah the prophet
Before the coming of the great and dreadful day of the LORD.
And he will turn
The hearts of the fathers to the children,
And the hearts of the children to their fathers,
Lest I come and strike the earth with a curse."
Malachi 4:5-6

This last statement of the Old Testament seems chilling in light of the reality that these were the last words recorded by the prophets for 400 years before the coming of Christ. These are the words carefully chosen by the God of the universe to leave with the human race before a unique period of silence. Of course, He has never been entirely silent. We know clearly during that time He was moving kings and setting up governments in preparation to receive the Messiah. The nations of the earth would be perfectly positioned for a baby to come into the world and change everything.

So why these words? Why not make a grand exit with

remarks about a coming majestic king or a display of His power or holy beauty? Why children and fathers? This is a question it would behoove us to ponder. If not simply because He said it, then perhaps because of the outcome promised if we don't.

"Lest I come and strike the land with a curse."

When I think of a curse, my mind immediately conjures up witches stirring up a big pot of poison and chanting an evil chorus. But that is not the type of curse Malachi is speaking of here. What is looming is a prophetic anathema, a divine denunciation. And I have to believe that as an exclamation point at the end of his letter, the prophet Malachi wasn't just talking about an isolated famine or even a plague. The warning in that last sentence of the Old Testament is much weightier, much more global than a local disaster. The Lord was warning His people that if they did not pay attention to His words, they would no longer hear His voice.

In searching the Scriptures for a worst case scenario of Biblical curses, I ran across an odd scene in Zechariah 5. Here, a scroll with a curse written on it is flying across the land, entering the houses of thieves and liars. The curse is banishment from the land. God will cut off the guilty and no longer allow access to the city. Being cut off from His Kingdom is truly the worst case scenario for God's people. If we do not heed the command to turn our hearts to the children of this generation, we are in danger of being cut off or expelled from His presence. This isn't just a "brass heaven" when we pray—you know the feeling, that your prayers are bouncing back unheard. No, this is expulsion from the Kingdom of God, access to the throne room being restricted because of disobedience.

Clearly, if we do not turn our hearts to the children in our day, we will not know the fullness of the Kingdom of God. Despite our prayers for revival and transformation of our nation, we will end up sitting outside of His promises if we do not act upon His prophetic command to embrace children.

So what does it look like for the church as a whole to "turn their hearts to the children"? To be honest, it's not easy to imagine a wholesale turning of the hearts. Even Christians are so consumed with their own destinies that at times it can be at the expense of, not because of, the next generation. When we look to the example of Christ, we see a clear picture of One who laid down His life for all humanity to become sons and daughters of God. He made a way at the cost of His own destiny and allowed His life to become the link to join the mortal with the eternal. By pondering His example, we get a glimpse of a heart that turns toward the generations to follow, those who will be the inheritance of Jesus when He returns. As the church embraces this corporate turning of the heart, something new will spring forth in our time. It will be the spirit of adoption manifesting in the lives of men, women and children, mirroring that which God has so graciously done for us.

The multifaceted wisdom of God is displayed in so many ways. When we live out this command to turn our hearts to the children, it will take many forms, with multiple expressions of His character. One such expression in our day is the act of adoption. Easton's Bible Dictionary describes adoption as "the giving to any one the name and place and privileges of a son who is not a son by birth." It is to this expression that we dedicate this book—adopting those without parents. Specifically adoption as a positive alternative to the abomination of abortion. Without expounding on the topic, abortion is the antithesis of the Malachi 4:6 command. Abortion is the cutting off of a life of hope and promise. For those who stand in the gap for life, adoption is an act of obedience and even prophecy in the face of the spirit of death. As we press into what the Lord has for us, He will pour out the spirit of adoption and drive back the curse of darkness.

As we pray for a mighty revival in America, asking for massive outpouring of His Spirit, we must realize that there is a required turning of the heart that corresponds with the outpouring. In Joel 2 we are promised that He will pour out His Spirit after there is a rending of the heart.

Malachi 4 is also a roadmap for revival in our day. He said He would send the prophets, or the "spirit of Elijah." That prophetic spirit would carry a message that would call for a great, multigenerational reconciliation in anticipation of the return of the Lord. The question is, how will we respond to this call?

Individually, we must release our own destiny into His hands for the sake of the next generation, striving to make "our ceiling their floor". Today's fathers and mothers are often too consumed with the fear of missing their own destiny to worry about the destiny of their own children. Those who can move beyond the fear of missing some great opportunity for the sake of their children are true heroes. One of those heroes is Therese Engle. As the wife of a well-known prophetic preacher, she could easily get caught up in the limelight of travel and recognition, but instead chooses to live in humility, insisting, "it's about me laying down my life so my children can succeed."

A church that is actively serving the children, the fatherless and the orphan is a precursor for revival to flow to our cities. Speaking about revival and the Kingdom of God, Allen Hood, Associate Director of the International House of Prayer, once said, "It's not about me anymore; it's about the next generation and what I can do to bring them up and make them great!"

As the hearts of the fathers turn to the children, God will make a way for the children to respond in like fashion, turning their hearts to their parents. What is coming is a wholesale family movement. The Church that remains at the end of the age will not be marked with the rebellion of youth or the heavy handedness of dysfunctional parenting. The family will stand as a unified body—perhaps for the first time since before Abel killed Cain and lied to his parents.

In this season that leads to the coming of Jesus, the heart of a Christian son or daughter needs to beat in sync with that of their father and mother. When Christian parents make the intentional syncing of these hearts a priority, we begin to join our voices with that of the Spirit, crying out "even so, Lord Jesus, come quickly." (Revelation 22:20.)

Turning our hearts toward the children is the art of becoming a son or daughter of the living God and extending sonship to the next generation, giving them wings to fly. As we lean into this challenge, we will find the rewards of His promises awaiting us. It is not God's desire to deliver a curse, but for His Kingdom to be displayed on the earth. He is simply looking for a people who will hear His voice and act. This is our time!

TWO

The New Underground Railroad

Adoption, by definition, is to legally bring a child into your family and raise that child as your own child. Some couples, eager to have a family but unable to conceive, choose adoption. Others see the plight of children who need a home and begin the adoption journey to provide these little ones with a forever family. These are both positive and valid reasons to adopt, but we want to issue the challenge to a third category of believers—those who perhaps have not thought of adoption before, but who are looking for a way to demonstrate a further commitment to justice as an expression of who they are in God. These are regular people on the outside, but revolutionaries on the inside. God is sounding a call in our day for revolutionaries who will look at adoption as an act of spiritual warfare and taking the Kingdom of God by force.

In January 2004, we packed up our family and headed to Washington, DC to help establish the Justice House of Prayer on Capitol Hill, a prayer room dedicated to praying for justice and righteousness to be restored to America. We specifically prayed for the ending of abortion each day by standing on the steps of the US Supreme Court in what we called a "silent siege". We were crying out for those in the womb who have no voice. It wasn't a protest, it was a prayer meeting. Standing in front of the US Supreme Court, we chose to take the issue of the unborn before the throne of God, the highest court in any land.

Depending on the day, we had between fifty and a hundred young people join us. As we stood in that place, hour upon hour, day after day, the Lord began to challenge us as a family.

What would happen if abortion ended in America? What would happen to those 4,500 babies that would be born each day rather than aborted? Would they be wanted? Would the Church step up to the task of caring for the orphan, the cast off ones, the unwanted? The harder question was, would we?

We had talked about adoption before we were married. You know, in those romantic days of dreaming together about what life would look like getting married and going forth to change the world—big crusades preaching the gospel, planting dozens of churches, traveling the globe for the sake of the Kingdom, and adopting orphans from the nations.

Yes, adoption was something we would do… someday. Of course, "someday" sat on the shelf like a glass vase that also came with the wedding, a beautiful reminder of those romantic days, but oh, so impractical. There were bills to pay and other things to do. Eventually, we began having biological children and the adoption dream got packed in a box with all the other memorabilia.

Eventually we had three sons, each spaced four years apart. We were fairly convinced we were done. We had done our part in populating the earth and could breathe a sigh of relief that the baby days were behind us. Besides, adoption seemed hard. We had heard the horror stories of exorbitant costs, long waiting periods and birth moms changing their minds. We already had biological children, so we were pretty sure we were disqualified for adoption here in the USA. We certainly didn't realize that there were babies born every day in this country who desperately needed a home to keep them from being lost in the "system". In our minds, domestic adoption was difficult; it took too long and was just too risky.

We couldn't have been more wrong. The Lord was about to take us on an incredible journey of discovery into the realm of adoption.

Late one night in Washington, D.C., we started talking with close friends about this radical idea of adopting a baby. We spoke in whispered tones as if we were afraid someone would overhear and call us crazy, when Brian Kim, a young man who had fasted and prayed through his college years for the ending of abortion, stood up and spoke to us with a fire in his eyes.

Brian, now a senior leader at the International House of Prayer in Kansas City, looked straight at us and boldly issued this charge: "Adoption is an extension of your intercession!"

That phrase resounded in our hearts like the sound of a great waterfall. The Lord was creating a roar within us to do what we believed was impossible. Still, we had our fears and were quick to vocalize them. "We don't have any money. Our house is so small. We don't have a vehicle big enough for a fourth child!"

Brian was ablaze with this idea and completely full of faith. In spite of our big objections, knowing that we had not filled out the first piece of paperwork and with no baby who was available for adoption, this young man immediately wrote us the first check for a "big vehicle" to hold all the children we would adopt one day. It's amazing to look back and see how the generation of twenty-somethings were the ones who, with great passion, spurred us on to believe the impossible.

In the weeks following that summer conversation in 2005, we simply could not shake the divine invitation to step out into an "extension of our intercession". We could pray daily standing before the mighty Supreme Court building. We could offer pious petitions in the secret place of devotion to the Lord, but He was showing us that as powerful as our words were before heaven, there was a tangible act of mercy that could answer our own prayers. Our intercession, invisible in the natural, would become a display of God's power and glory to shift paradigms in the nation.

In our dreaming and praying, we began to see how adoption is an active, tangible means of spiritual warfare. The posture of war is not sitting back and waiting for something to happen—it's aggressive, unrelenting taking the Kingdom by force. It's certainly not for the faint of heart. Fortunately, when believers are weak, there is strength in standing in partnership with Jesus, contending for the children to be set in families.

I'll never forget the morning that we were contending for our twins. Randy had heard about newborn twin girls in Florida who needed a family. We were sitting at a coffee shop a few hours later, Blackberries buzzing as we made calls to lawyers, social workers and the birth mother, trying to make last minute arrangements. For a while, it didn't look like anyone wanted to help us, and every minute that went by put us another minute closer to the twins going into foster care.

Suddenly, the thought occurred to me that I needed to pray and win this battle in the heavenly realm. I got up from the table and walked toward the parking lot, boldly telling the Lord that I wanted Him to intervene and work out the details for those baby girls to be our own. It was in that moment I felt the very direct invitation from the Holy Spirit, as if He was saying, "OK, they are yours. Now fight for them!"

I went into full-blown intercession right there in the middle of the coffee shop parking lot. Something shifted in my spirit and I could feel that we were in a battle for the very lives of these babies, and somehow that battle depended on my prayers. I got aggressive, claiming them as our daughters, declaring their lives as an inheritance for Jesus. After a few minutes, I felt I was done. I walked back to the table, confident something had been accomplished in the spirit realm that would now manifest in the physical. Sure enough, we had secured an attorney. Additionally, the social worker and the hospital agreed that they would hold these girls for us until we could get there. We went forward with the practical details of airline tickets, hotel reservations and all the other necessary arrangements. Deep in my spirit I knew that these children weren't won in the details, they were won in our hearts as we partnered with the God of heaven to rescue them and set them in a family—His family (Psalm 68).

We are certainly not the first people to have these thoughts. Both the present day and our history are full of people who were not content to hold their convictions; they wanted to act on them.

From the very conception of our nation, there was an idea that perhaps some men and women were not fully human. It's hard to explain the thought process behind slavery—much of it was financially motivated—but it rested on the idea that one human being's body might be the property of another.

This idea was quantified by the Three Fifths Compromise made in the Philadelphia Convention of 1787, when southern states wanted to use their large population of slaves to account for the number of delegates they demanded in the US House of Representatives.

By using the slaves to increase their population, slave owners received more representation at the federal level. Then, by not allowing slaves to vote, the slave owners would get an even greater percentage of representation. Northern states, who wouldn't benefit from the same arrangement, agreed instead to what became known as the "Federal Ratio of Three Fifths", meaning that the life of a slave counted as 3/5 of that of a white man. It was the first instance of a federally recognized standard indicating blacks were officially less than human.

The issue festered for decades, with those on both sides pressing for some sort of final resolve in a manner most favorable to them. Those in the South wanted expansion of slavery throughout the West. For opposite reasons, representatives from the North, like John Quincy Adams, refused to let the issue rest.

With the Three Fifths Compromise seemingly settling the issue in the courts, slavery remained so contentious that by 1856, a pro-abolition speech by Massachusetts Senator Charles Sumner enraged South Carolina Representative Preston Brooks. Two days later, he approached Sumner in the Senate chamber and beat him senseless with a gold-headed cane until Sumner was blind from his own blood, and Brooks' cane broke over Sumner's head. Brooks stormed out of the chamber in a huff and later received a number of canes in the mail from fellow South Carolinians to replace the one he broke during the beating.

In that inflamed atmosphere, where the very mention of slavery might bring a beating upon a man in the political arena, there was a secondary movement, an undercover network of people that didn't confront slavery in the public arena but chose to do something about it. They didn't wave signs, they didn't yell and they often didn't even make their beliefs public. They simply worked behind the scenes to see men set free.

This system was known as the Underground Railroad. The Underground Railroad was loosely organized around a few very key beliefs, the primary one being that no human should be subject to the horrors of slavery. Slaves in the South who could muster the courage to run would find help in the way of ordinary Americans known as conductors. These conductors were responsible for getting escaped slaves to the next stop on their journey to being free, often risking life, limb and fortune to move strangers from captivity to freedom. In most cases they would never know the names of those they were rescuing, much less know what came of them after they left their care. But, to these tireless workers, it was worth it.

Through this system of underground stations—caves, barns, guest homes and boat rides that led to the North—thousands found freedom even as the battle raged about whether or not they deserved it. While some saw fit to argue, others saw fit to act, and in those actions, the system of slavery was undermined with each one brought out to freedom.

A similar situation arose in 1973, when the US Supreme Court determined that the right of a woman to terminate the life of her child superseded the right of the child to life itself. In a sense, the child was ruled to be property rather than an individual itself, and, like the slave owner of old, the woman could do what she would with her property. Whether it was one fourth human, half human or three fifths human was not the point. The point was that the child was less than fully human, and, in that case, the rights of the 'fully human' woman became preeminent.

As contentious as slavery was in the 1800's, the issue of abortion raises as much or more anger on both sides of the issue. While we honor those who have lovingly held to the standard of life beginning at conception, thirty plus years after *Roe* v. *Wade*, the law still stands, and the murder of children remains legal in the land. We are appealing for a corresponding, parallel movement that will open the door to life for countless babies slated for death.

Adoption is to abortion what the Underground Railroad was to slavery.

Quietly behind the scenes, every day people work to make safe places for these children that some would consider less than human. Social workers, attorneys, doctors and adoption professionals work to help birth mothers down a path to a better life for their baby and themselves.

Part of the reason that federally protected freedom was so slow in coming to the slaves was the question of what to do with millions of slaves throughout the South if they were all to be set free. As embarrassed as they were to admit it, even many staunch abolitionists in the North did not want their cities full of freed blacks, and so they withheld vocal support for a wholesale emancipation. While the church has been highly vocal in its opposition to abortion, it has largely failed to think about what it means if we get our way. We're in favor of the concept of saving babies, but when our church halls and foyers are full of 4 year olds, are we still as pro-life as we were when holding the signs?

We are in need of another abolitionist movement that will be a part of the answer to the question, "What are we going to do with all these babies?" We need mothers and fathers willing to open their arms. We need doctors and lawyers willing to discount their services. We need pastors with the intestinal fortitude to challenge their congregations with this question, "If we are able to save the babies, will you help them find freedom?"

The conductors moved the slaves from one safe house to another. Each house offered a meal, a bed, and a few hours of respite from the run. It was disruptive to everyday life for a person to serve as a conductor or to operate a safe house. Slaves came at all hours of the night, ate precious food and often needed clean clothing or disguises.

Being a conductor on the Underground Railroad was a thankless and often dangerous job. Their passengers came to you tired, needy and fearful. Because of their passengers' troubled life and experiences, a conductor often had to both win the trust of the passengers as well as move them along to freedom.

In this way, adoption is not much different from freeing slaves. It's hard work. It's inconvenient. It's costly. It's far easier to simply give verbal ascent to the idea of being pro-life than it is to prepare to be a safe house and take in those for whom we are praying to be set free.

> *In operating the adoption agency that we direct, we regularly have people who want to volunteer to help. I have a standard conversation I go through with prospective volunteers, asking them, "Why do you want to help at an adoption agency?" As you would expect, the answer is often, "I like babies..."*
>
> *Without trying to be overly discouraging, I firmly tell them, "You could feasibly serve at the adoption agency office for a long time and never see a baby. Adoption from this angle is made up of difficult pieces of paper that need to be filled out perfectly in triplicate and reviewed by an unknown person who will only call you to tell you that you did it wrong. There is very little recognition outside of our office. We can't talk about our successes because of confidentiality issues. This is a labor of love, but it is not necessarily about singing lullabies or changing diapers."*
>
> *It's not that I intentionally want to discourage anyone, but I do want to drive home the same thing that we tell adoptive families—that adoption alternates between tedium and warfare, only occasionally touching on the cute and cuddly. We do it because we want children, and because we want to help children, but in doing it we recognize, like the underground railroad conductors, that it is not primarily about our needs or desires. It is about another human being finding his or her way to life.*

No one better understands the cost of redemption than Jesus Himself. He came to Earth with no rosy notions of parades or accolades. Admittedly, He saw some of those, but they ultimately led to His death on a cross. It's the ultimate irony that the true Messiah fully had none of the characteristics that usually result in people being diagnosed with having a Messiah Complex. He had no romantic idea of what He was called to do. He fully understood that His role in the redemption of man necessitated that He lay down His life. He is now looking for people willing to lay down theirs—if not literally, then figuratively, in the way of surrendering their comfort, their finances and their status quo in hope that others might find life.

Because it is the way of God to use human beings to accomplish His purposes, God is looking for people who will help build this underground railroad for the unborn. He is searching to and fro for those whose hearts are fully His, and when He finds them, He helps them find their place on the route.

Most commonly the first person on the route to freedom is a counselor at a women's clinic or crisis pregnancy center. Often located right next to an abortion clinic, these clinics are the first line of defense against abortion. Once inside, a women learns that life is indeed an alternative to death. She see her child for the first time on an ultrasound screen, and something shifts in her spirit. That which the woman thought was a blob becomes a baby before her very eyes. When the worker sees a glimmer of hope, she helps the woman make a plan for life, and often steers her in the direction of an adoption agency, the next stop on the underground railroad.

Most agencies provide services, referrals to medical help, and compassionate professionals who guide the birth mothers through the process. Our agency has several people on staff who are degreed, licensed professionals on the surface but clearly intercessors below the surface. We meet weekly to pray for specific birth moms, adoptive families and others, as well as favor in the eyes of the legal authorities and others involved. These professionals are clearly conductors on the underground railroad, making connections and moving infants along from the dangerous designation of unborn to the arms of a loving family.

Others conductors are midwives who pray with birth moms as they make the difficult but godly choice for life. They approach the issue from the perspective of the medical community and make sure that birth moms and babies are cared for holistically, being made well physically, mentally and spiritually.

Some will open their very homes and hearts, taking tremendous risks in doing so, in order that God might set the lonely and unwanted in families. They house birth moms while they are preparing to have their babies, offering some of these girls the first safe place they've had to rest their head in many, many months.

Finally, there are the families who make the commitment that goes far beyond nine months. They make a place in their homes and their lives for a new little one, committing to love and care for that child as their very own. They give their money, their time and their very name to ensure this child knows she was wanted from the start.

Of this we are certain: the need for a new Underground Railroad is so great that for those who want a place on the route, a place can be found. It may be helping in the crisis pregnancy clinic, in the hospital, in the agency, in the adoptive home, or as a volunteer anywhere along the way. To win the freedom of a generation under siege, we desperatcly need help... and there is a spot for you.

THREE

The Battle for the Children

Our third son, Zion, took a bit of a turn on us when he was seven years old. It wasn't a turn for the worse or the better, it was simply a facet of his personality that we hadn't fully recognized.

Our quiet son had spent an hour or two nearly every day playing a guitar. He started at two years old with little cardboard cutouts. He moved on to stringed toy guitars, then actual small guitars. Eventually, he started beating on things: Pots, pans, tables, his car seat. He was a guitar player and a drummer. We had a musician; it was obvious. However, when we signed him up for soccer, we discovered there was a lot more to him than the little drummer boy. Zion the musician became Zion the warrior, and the soccer field was his battlefield.

We actually missed his first game, as we were on our way to Florida to adopt our twins. I received a phone call from one of the other dads during the game asking me, "What happened to your boy?"

"Why do you say that?" I replied.

"You need to see him play soccer... he's an animal!"

Zion plays soccer with more animation than anyone I've ever seen. There is no tentativeness about him. He walks on to the field like a man who owns the ground. He throws his small frame into the fray with such enthusiasm that he's left more than one much bigger player laying on the ground wondering what truck hit him, as Zion moved the ball further down the field. Shoulder length hair streaming behind him and a wild look in his eye, all that is missing to turn him into a full-on Braveheart character is a little face paint and a Scottish accent... and if we let him paint his face for games, he'd probably go for it.

Fall and spring for Zion, the soccer field is the battlefield. It's the same way for children across the nation. They line up, they yell with all the fierceness that their little voices can convey, and they do battle. Then, they line up and eat orange slices after the game.

There is another battle raging involving children. It's not fought by the children, but it's fought for the children. It's not for bragging rights at the ice cream stand; it's for the destiny of a generation, and beyond that, for the destiny of the human race. Because each side fully understands that to win the children is to win the future.

Historically, whenever a deliverer was about to come on the scene, there was a battle against the children.

In spite of controlling the food supply, the weapons, the political clout and the military might of a massive army, Pharaoh somehow sensed the potential in the Hebrew children. He looked at those slaves with straw and dung on their hands, and he worried that one day a deliverer would rise from among them. In that situation, he had options. He could have vanquished the obvious leaders from the Hebrews. He could have tortured the men or separated the married couples to create havoc, but he didn't. In abject fear of the future, he waged war on the children.

Pharaoh met with the midwives who helped with the birth of the Hebrew children and gave the following order: "When the Hebrew women give birth, if the baby is a boy, kill him."

Economically, this was a bad idea. Within a generation, under Pharaoh's plan, his slave labor base would be emaciated. His army of Hebrew brick makers would be populated entirely by women who wouldn't be bearing children because there would be no Hebrew men to father them. Interestingly, Pharaoh was so scared of a deliverer rising that he was willing to kill off the strength of the people rather than see them rebel. He felt he could afford to kill them, but he couldn't afford to allow them to dream of a life of their own.

Of course, things don't always go the way that dictators wish, particularly when the hand of God is in the mix.

There was a baby born to a Levite. Scripture says he was a beautiful child. The details of how he escaped the hand of the midwife are not clear, but he remained hidden by his mother for three months. The story says that at some point, it became very difficult to hide him. At three months of age, he probably cried a little louder and moved around a little more and so his mother feared for her life and for the life of her child. She sent the baby with her daughter, who placed him in basket near the edge of the river, and stepped away to watch from a distance.

In a storyline that only God could orchestrate, that baby was discovered by Pharaoh's own daughter. She must have had a compassionate heart. The Bible says she wept when she saw the baby—perhaps with joy, perhaps in relief, knowing that in the current political state, it was extremely dangerous to be a Hebrew baby. For whatever reason, she felt pity for this child and brought him home.

She named him Moses, and from that baby boy, God fashioned a deliverer for the Hebrew people. Within the house of Pharaoh, a deliverer grew stronger every day. He lived in the very palace that had called for the war against the children, and yet the adoption spared the life of this deliverer to come.

Some years later, long after Moses' death, the Jewish people found themselves enslaved once again. They had left Egypt, wandered through the desert and eventually found their way to the Promised Land, only to be carried off in captivity to Babylon. Into that captivity, a young girl was born.

Hadassah—or Esther—was an orphan. Her parents died when she was still very young. It was a difficult time for a young slave girl without family attachments. Male slaves were used for building projects, but young female slaves, particularly those with no men to protect them, were probably used for other things.

In that situation, even though another child meant another mouth to feed, her cousin Mordecai took her under his wing. The Bible says he raised her as his daughter. He adopted Esther, and in doing so, earned himself influence for the future that he could never have fully understood at the time.

As a teenager, Esther found herself an unlikely queen. The pagan king was pleased with her beauty and chose her to be his wife. The little orphan girl was now in a place of privilege. No one in the King's court knew her true secret; the beautiful queen of Babylon was in reality a slave girl. The man who had the greatest influence over her was not her King-Husband, but a despised Jewish man. That man was a political target of the King's court, yet he could speak into the Queen's heart and move her to action because he had adopted her when she was helpless and vulnerable.

As time went by, a plot arose to kill the Jews. In that moment, Mordecai spoke quickly to Queen Esther. He warned her against thinking that perhaps marrying into the royal court of the enemy afforded her more protection than being an adopted daughter of a Jewish man. He implored her to speak to the King on behalf of her people, and when she balked, he pointed out that this was an opportunity of epic proportion. "If you remain completely silent at this time," he said, "relief and deliverance will arise for the Jews from another place, but you and your father's house will perish. Yet who knows whether you have come to the Kingdom for such a time as this?" (Esther 4:14)

The influence of a cousin-turned-adoptive-father was enough to inspire Esther's heart to stand for righteousness and to turn the heart of the king. The influence of her adoptive father set in motion a series of events including Mordecai's enemy being hung on the gallows that the enemy had prepared for Mordecai. The influence of an adoptive father pressed Esther to win freedom for her people and gave Mordecai such renown among their captors that the Bible says "many people among them became Jews." In a sense, Mordecai's influence did not just save the Jewish people, it served to open the door of salvation even to those who held them in slavery. Esther, an adopted Jewish girl, followed in Moses' steps as an adoptee raised up to be a deliverer.

There was another man born without a father. His mother was engaged to a man named Joseph, but he was not the father. Any normal man would have distanced himself from the girl and been justified in doing so, except that Joseph had received a message from an angel early on in the pregnancy, and the angel gave him clear direction about this child.

This was not a child conceived by an errant fiancé in a one-night stand. This was not an embarrassment. Shame was not the destiny of this child. No, He would be a deliverer. Jesus needed a father figure on earth that could protect His mother, raise Him properly, and teach Him a trade.

Joseph did those things. He offered a name and a home to Mary and this Son of hers. He played with him, chased Him among the olive trees, and even scolded Him when, at twelve years old, Jesus got sidetracked teaching in the temple and could not be found. He taught Jesus how to work with His hands, how to saw timbers and how to hold nails. One can't help but wonder, when working in His father's shop, if Jesus ever held a nail with a bit of foresight as to why He was born.

Joseph wholeheartedly adopted the Son of God, and in doing so, played a role in the salvation of the human race.

Historically, whenever the enemy feels a certain urgency, he chooses to wage war against the biggest threat, that is, the children. Afraid that his days may be coming to an end, he unleashes an unholy fury against the weakest among us, seeking either to kill them outright or to gain such a grip over them that they are forever in his grasp.

To this day, the enemy seeks to influence or kill children outright. It is his primary scheme to influence the outcome of the events of the future.

Throughout Asia, you can find countless Buddhist orphanages built within monasteries. Under the watchful eye of orange-clad Buddhist priests or within the sounds of flapping Buddhist prayer flags, children laugh and play. It looks innocuous at first glance— who can argue with people caring for children—until you realize that the Buddhist priesthood is significantly populated by adult orphans who have been raised in the orphanages and stay to carry on the work simply because they know no way but Buddha. The dark spirits behind Buddhism know that if they target children, they will own the nations of Tibet, Cambodia, Thailand and others for generations to come.

The battle for the children is not localized. It does not stay far across the ocean and leave us to live our lives in America. It's being fought here, and in some circles, even Christians are so calloused to it they wonder if the children are a cause worth defending.

In 1973, a declaration of war was issued in the form of a US

Supreme Court ruling entitled *Roe* v. *Wade*. With that edict, it became the law of the land that a mother who chose or was coerced to end the life of her child could do so without a reason. After nearly thirty years of carnage, seeing over 50,000,000 babies murdered, Congress made a half-hearted attempt to bring some sanity to the process by enacting the Partial Birth Abortion Ban, which would stop a particularly brutal process of aborting babies nearly up to the date they should have been born.

Three US District Courts were so bent on maintaining the assault on children that they found the ban unconstitutional. Eventually, the US Supreme Court did uphold the very narrow ban on a few types of abortion late in pregnancy—but even then, it did so by one vote. America decided to spare a few of her children an agonizing death by the slim margin of one single vote. That is how hot the battle is raging against this generation. That is how fearful the enemy is. Having some sense of the destiny of a generation yet to be born, he fights with all his power to prevent as many as possible to ever taste life outside the womb.

Approximately 1 in 3 pregnancies—intended or otherwise—ends in doctor-administered death before the child takes its first breath, but 2 in 3 are born. Those that are born into circumstances where a mother is unable or unwilling to parent them face the enemy's second line of defense. They go into a foster care system or directly to be adopted.

However, one of the fastest growing segments of adoption are those that place children with gay or lesbian couples. A simple internet search will reveal agencies nationwide that not only allow homosexuals to adopt but also market their services directly to the homosexual community. You'll find web pages congratulating "Steve and John on the birth of their son". Unable to have children by normal means and desperately wanting the trappings of a 'normal family' in order to more integrate themselves into society, homosexual couples extend their influence through adoption.

To a nominal Christian or a person with no spiritual understanding, it would seem to be a good thing that these two loving individuals have taken a child into their home, but what is really happening in the spirit realm? A child is being given over to a home where immorality is touted as a viable option. The lifestyle that will be portrayed to that child is an aberration before the Lord. Not having known anything different, how is that child ever to find sexual normalcy at adulthood? Having survived the crucial months within the womb, the child is now relegated to an upbringing that serves as a secondary attack on their psyche and development.

The battle for the children became an internationally public issue on January 12, 2010, as the tectonic plates that met below the Caribbean ocean floor suddenly slipped under tremendous pressure. One end of the island of Hispaniola was rocked and in the course of a few minutes, Haiti lay in ruins.

Even before the quake, Haiti was a land of scarcity, not plenty. There was little infrastructure. There was little in the way of medicine. There was often not enough food or clean water. What Haiti does have, however, is a lot of children. Most of the population is under fifteen years of age. In the good days, before the quake, these children played communally in the streets. In the minutes, weeks, and now months following the quake, they wander the slums and tent cities looking for family or friends. Most of them do not find what they're looking for.

Immediately, the battle for the children became apparent. There were three groups of people who were vying for the children and they all stepped into high gear.

The first was the government, who in years past had never really done a good job of tracking orphans or caring for them. The adoption process served to grease the pockets of officials and was dragged out as long as possible to keep wealthy Americans and Europeans paying to care for their Haitian adoptive children by keeping them in the country. The government often treated these children as one of their most profitable industries. The idea that they may lose control of this asset struck fear in the hearts of bureaucrats across Haiti.

The second group was Christians around the world. Many had been trying to do effective ministry in Haiti for years. Others were new to the country. Some were well versed in Creole and Haitian culture. Others were ham-fisted in their approach with little understanding of the people. Still, they meant well and brought both dollars and open arms. In some cases they wanted to care for the children on site, repairing orphanages and building new ones. More commonly, they wanted to help speed the adoption process to get children into the homes of families who could care for them in the USA and Europe. This caused great fear in the hearts of the Haitian government, who, under encouragement from the United Nations, immediately shut down all new adoptions and made those in process so complex that many people slept in the US Embassy for days until their papers cleared, being told over and over "yes" only to hear "no" from another official. Christians, for the most part, played by the rules, which is to say they re-calibrated their efforts to care for Haitian children without removing them from the country.

The third group was not bound by the rules of Christian charity or legal standards. They were unconcerned by national laws or the United Nations; they were coming for illegal reasons anyway. They were the child traffickers who, in anticipation of the chaos that would follow the earthquake, immediately gathered from around the world to sneak children over the border into the Dominican Republic or off the shores of Haiti itself to boats that lie in wait.

This three way tug of war for the children between the state, the church, and the traffickers best illustrates the sort of battle that will be waged at the end of the age. Those who feel the responsibility for children's well-being belongs to the government will argue for state control. Others who profit by selling these children as sex slaves will gather up as many as they can. Standing firmly against both of these groups will be the church of Jesus, and in accordance with God's great plan, that church is waking up to the plight of orphans like never before.

While we are sobered by this battle for the children, we are not without hope. We are beginning to see pockets of movement as places here and there begin to understand that children are not simply those who show up for VBS every year, but the very children of God.

These faith communities are banding together to support adoption and orphan care both here in the US and around the world. Pastors like Bishop W.C. Martin in Possum Trot, Texas are challenging their people to walk out their faith—with a church of 200 members, Bishop Martin led his people to adopt over 70 children in a very short amount of time. What a story of redemption from this amazing community!

There is a rapidly growing awareness of the need to adopt and how it fits into the life of a believer. People are beginning to look at it as a part of the Great Commission. Adoption conferences are being held all over the nation and drawing record crowds. These conferences are focusing on how the gospel is lived out through adoption and why it should be a vital part of any healthy church.

Most importantly, on a micro level, young couples are standing up to the lie that a third car or extra week of vacation would make them happy. Instead, they're investing their extra time and income into embracing children who would not otherwise have a home. They are taking their place on the battlefront and saying, "We will not surrender our futures to our convenience—give us the children."

This, of course, is only the beginning. There will be a great eschatological adoption movement at the end of the age. Even a cursory study of end time events will reveal wars, disasters and judgments that will kill a significant percentage of human beings. This will lead to a huge number of orphans wandering the face of the earth, looking for a home. The church of Jesus will rise to the occasion and embrace this border-less nation of children. In doing so, the children's needs will be met and the cause of Jesus will be moved forward as a generation learns that God is their ultimate father and He will fight for them.

Even now, facing what we feel is great resistance, the church is finding its voice in the battle for children. Sobered as we are, we remember that like so many other great battles in history, this one belongs to the Lord.

FOUR

The Great Finalization

The process of adoption is full of terms that you may not have heard or may not have understood if you haven't gone through the process. When we began our journey, we had a rough understanding of what a home study was, but we had no clue how to interpret some of the legal jargon. There was one term that we were able to figure out on our own though because we loved the sound of it: *finalization*. We may not have fully comprehended all that went into it, but we knew what it meant. Upon finalization, the adoption was complete and irrevocable. We longed for finalization when we adopted both Zoe and our twins, Anna and Mercy.

Even though the child is wholly adopted into your heart the moment you embrace him or her, there are certain formalities to walk out. You must fill out paperwork, file documents with the court, and have a series of follow up meetings with social workers who ensure that the child is doing well. Eventually, a judge signs all the paperwork which makes what has already happened in your heart a legal reality. This day often resembles a court proceeding, a christening, and a birthday party all rolled into one.

We finalized Zoe's adoption in a family courtroom in the midtown area of Kansas City. The lobby was full of people waiting to see a judge and have their cases heard. There were two distinct groups of people in the waiting area. Some families, like ours, were preparing to have their adoptions finalized. They were excited and smiling, many already making plans to celebrate with a special lunch as soon as the proceedings were over. Others were not there for a happy reason. When not finalizing adoptions, the family court deals with custody issues. It was not hard to tell who was in what group; you could see the hope and joy in some eyes and the pain and despair in others.

We were probably more nervous going into that finalization hearing than we were our wedding ceremony. We had our three sons in tow. Each was dressed in his finest, unwilling to miss this event and fully prepared to answer questions from the judge. Suddenly, our name was called and we were ushered in before the bench.

Television has shaped most of our perceptions about courtrooms, and most of what we have learned is wrong. Most courtrooms are not grand affairs with ornate woodwork, tall ceilings and seating for a hundred people. In this case, the room was slightly larger than our living room. At one end sat a judge behind a raised desk. In the middle of the room was a table where we were directed to sit. A woman we'd never met before was introduced to us as our daughters' court appointed lawyer.

After making a few perfunctory remarks, the judge got down to business. In essence, he invited our lawyer to make a case for this child to be placed permanently in our family.

We were asked to state our names and a few specific details about what we did for a living and where we lived. Then, the lawyer asked a series of questions:

"Do you believe you will be able to financially provide for this child?"

"Yes, sir."

"Do you commit to being her father and mother?"

"Yes sir."

"Do you accept full responsibility for this child as if she were one of your naturally born children?" he asked.

"Yes, sir."

"Do you understand that this proceeding is full, complete and irrevocable?"

Hot tears burned in our eyes as we croaked out a "Yes".

Did we understand? Was he kidding? This was the day we had lived for. All we wanted was for this little one to be recognized for who she was—our daughter. After a moment of deliberation, the judge announced "Petition granted!" and signed the papers in a flurry. In minutes we were back out in the waiting area, boys cheering, parents crying, and a little girl who now had a forever family and a new identity.

The twins' finalization was different. We'd received a phone call from the Florida court clerk in early December saying "The judge realizes you're scheduled to finalize the adoption of your girls in January, but he realizes there are some tax advantages to finalizing in December. Would you be interested in doing the finalization on December 31st?"

Of course we were interested, but our family was supposed to be at a conference on December 31st. The clerk assured us that there was nothing to worry about—we could do the whole thing over the phone. We were told to call a certain number in the presence of a notary at 9:30 a.m., December 31st, 2008.

That morning, with the hotel accountant (who was also a notary) looking on, we used a conference room phone to dial the number the clerk had given us.

I swallowed hard as the phone rang, unsure of what to expect.
I'd only talked to a judge a few times in my life, and never over

the phone. I anticipated hearing the voice of James Earl Jones. Instead, the man who answered sounded more like Deputy Dog.

"Ha-lo!" he answered. "This is the judge!"

My eyes opened wide as the hotel notary's head jerked up to look at me. She was beginning to wonder if this was real. I had to admit, so was I. "Hello, Your Honor," I replied. "This is Randy Bohlender, I'm gathered here with my wife, Kelsey, our twins, and a notary for finalization."

"Of course!" he said happily, and then chatted for a moment about the weather before asking how the girls were doing. We assured him they were doing well. With a casual nature, he asked us a variation of the same questions we'd been asked during Zoe's finalization. Within a few minutes, he finished up and announced, "I am signing… the… papers… right now! Mr. and Mrs. Bohlender, these two little girls are forever named Anna River Bohlender and Mercy Rain Bohlender. They are forever yours."

We cried. The judge congratulated us. The notary smiled. In less than ten minutes we were out in the lobby and our girls had new names—names that we had called them since birth, but now no one could deny who they were. They were ours. No longer was there any amount of fear, loneliness, or angst about what might happen. They had new names.

These proceedings didn't just mark the end of a process. They were far more profound than that. In all three girls' cases, they had been named at birth by their birth mothers. We are incredibly grateful for the brave women who carried our three girls to full term, especially in a culture that makes abortion so easy. They loved as well as they knew how—which is all that any of us can do, really. Nevertheless, they carried with them a lot of pain and spiritual baggage. There was depression, fear, anxiety, and even some drug use. Intentionally or not, all of this went into their naming the girls. They named their daughters according to the spirit that ruled them. While the names were not vile or shaming, they were the names given them under a different spiritual authority than the ones they were now under. We knew from the beginning that we would give them new names.

We never once used the names that their birth mothers had given them. We always called them Zoe, Anna River and Mercy Rain. The twins' adoption happened so quickly that we had them out of the hospital and in a hotel room for 2 days before we could figure out what to name them. Even then we didn't resort to using the names the birth mother had given them. We prayed, we talked, and we prayed some more, knowing that we couldn't call them "this one" and "that one" forever!

Even though we never called them by their given names— few people on the earth even know what those names are—the reality was that while they were our girls in our hearts, there remained for each of them a document with a name on it that would have led you to think otherwise. Somewhere buried in a courtroom file cabinet, there was a birth certificate, a hospital file or a social worker's case notes that used their old names.

In those finalization proceedings, they were officially given their new names. We remember leaving Zoe's new birth certificate on our kitchen whiteboard for weeks after posting it there for her finalization party. Next to the corrected birth certificate Kelsey had written with a fat, black marker, "Revelation 2:17: I will give him a white stone, and on the stone a new name written which no one knows except him who receives it."

We loved walking by that piece of paper held in place by fridge magnets and seeing Zoe's new name, wiping out the last symbolic tie to any time when she might not have been wanted or considered ours. Sometimes, with no one in the room, we would read it out loud just to hear it. We were declaring the will of the courts and adding our own amen for good measure. This girl was ours.

So much of the adoption process points to the things of the spirit. It is no accident that God uses the metaphor of adoption to describe how we become a part of His family.

> *Romans 8:14-15: "For as many as are led by the Spirit of God, these are the sons of God. For you did not receive the spirit of bondage again to fear, but you received the Spirit of adoption by whom we cry out, 'Abba, Father'."*

None of us have a birth certificate declaring God to be our Father, nevertheless He has made Himself just that. He chose us. We were not born His, but we become His through the miracle of adoption.

This adoption was not a spur of the moment decision. Since the moment Adam and Eve sinned in the Garden, God knew that something would have to be done to redeem the lives of those He already loved so much.

> *Galatians 4:4-5: "But when the fullness of time had come, God sent forth His Son, born of a woman, born under the law, to redeem those that were under the law, that we might receive the adoption as sons."*

There is an innate desire in the hearts of men and women to be identified as sons and daughters of someone. No one wants to be an orphan at any age.

For some time we've been involved with TheCall, a series of corporate solemn assemblies of prayer and fasting for our nation. Since 2000, TheCall gatherings have been held on the National Mall in Washington, D.C., the San Diego Chargers stadium, and a dozen venues in between.

Nearly 20,000 people gathered for TheCall Kansas City on December 31, 2007 for a day of repentance and crying out to God on behalf of our nation. That afternoon, as we stood backstage helping manage stage traffic, worship leader Jason Upton led the crowd in a song he'd written that highlights this unique adoptive relationship we have with God.

Though there are several verses, it's the chorus that brought the crowd to a crescendo. For nearly twenty minutes, first with the band playing, and then no musical accompaniment at all, the 20,000 lifted their voices singing, "Sons and daughters of the living God... Sons and daughters of the living God."

No matter what is happening onstage during these events, the backstage area can be a beehive of activity. Radios crackle, equipment is moved, and people mill around waiting to go on stage or having just come off. For most of that twenty minute period, though, almost all activity ceased. It was as if the physical world was tentative of interrupting the Spirit.

As the crowd sang the refrain over and over, "Sons and daughters of the living God..." we found ourselves listening through the black fabric stage backdrop. TheCall has known some historic moments with larger crowds in more epic venues, but no moment has ever matched the enthusiasm that seemed to come out of the very depths of those gathered in that crowded event hall. It very well may have been the loudest that the assembled crowd had been all day. They sang loudly and unreservedly, because that one lyric illustrated all they ever wanted: to be a son or a daughter of the living God.

The groaning of their hearts to be sons and daughters is described in the Bible.

Romans 8:22-23: "For we know that the whole creation groans and labors with birth pangs together until now. Not only that, but we also who have the first fruits of the Spirit, even we ourselves groan within ourselves, eagerly waiting for the adoption, the redemption of our body."

As believers, we are all anxiously awaiting the finalization of our own adoption into the family of God. That's not to negate or downplay what He's done in redeeming us thus far. The moment we respond in accepting God's grace, we are changed. The Bible says that we become a new creation at that moment. Becoming a child of God is an instantaneous, glorious work of grace, but many still struggle with identity, with a propensity to sin, and a tendency to reflect the nature with which we were born.

We are fully saved and yet there is an element of finalization that we long for. That longing is reflective of an inward knowledge of a coming age. There is a day coming when our process of adoption comes to a grand finale.

The book of Revelation speaks of the great Day of the Lord when all history culminates in the coming of the King. He is coming to bring justice to the earth and in a very real sense, to finalize the adoption He initiated in our hearts. Our adoption finalization is marked by our receiving a new name that only God knows to call us because only God can see what we shall be on that day.

Though we long for this finalization, we still struggle with the dichotomy of knowing we are a son or daughter of God while still legally being a resident of the current age. We know the love of the Father, but we process it through an identity of one who remembers too much pain and sorrow to fully comprehend what has happened to us through adoption. In this age, we know in part and understand in part, but we will understand fully when He comes. On that day when the King returns, we will no longer be known as lonely, frightened, angry or defeated. Isaiah 25:8 prophesies of a day when He will wipe away every tear and make all things right. Truly, all things will become new.

Much has been made of the idea of "going to heaven". As

children, many of us were told that would be the end of all days. We were never given a lot of details but assumed it involved some harp playing and cloud riding. We smiled and pretended to be excited. Inwardly, we wondered, "Is that all there is?"

This idea of escaping to a cloud sells short the full plan of God, which is not that we all go to heaven, but rather that heaven comes to earth. Ephesians 1:9-10 promises that He'll make known to us the mystery of His will, which will come into fulfillment as He brings all things in heaven and on earth together under one head even Christ.

Romans 8:17 (NIV) goes on to say, "If we are His children, then we are heirs—heirs of God and co-heirs with Christ, if indeed we share in His sufferings in order that we may also share in His glory." He's not making a way for us to escape this realm, He's preparing to reign over the nations and invites us to join Him! He will rule the earth in righteousness and justice and we will serve at His side.

Knowing this, what do we do now? As we all wait for that great day, adoption in the natural is an act of Kingdom prophecy. With each movement of the heart, faithfully committing to give a child a home, a family and a future, we prophesy what God has done for us. Adoption shouts life, love, eternity and the Kingdom of God. It speaks louder than protest signs or legislation. It shouts to the world, "We want the babies!" The selfless act of granting life and love to a child communicates even to the principalities and powers of this present age, displaying the manifold wisdom of God in mirroring His love and redemptive purposes for humanity. It's what Christ died for: to give us a new life, a new name and an eternal glory.

The God of all creation is looking for those who will be a part of this movement and prophesy about a good Father to all the world.

FIVE

Giving and Receiving Life

*E*rin *couldn't believe this was happening to her. She knew*
she was on a bad path—certainly not the one her family and
friends had hoped for. She'd struggled with the results of her bad
decisions for a while now, but she surely didn't see it coming to
this. This was more than unexpected. This was unthinkable.

A popular student at a Christian high school, Erin had found
it easy to make friends when she moved on to a Christian
college. Her razor sharp wit and good looks seemed to make
a way for her, but not all the doors that opened to her led to
things that were good. There were bad influences, and in some
cases, just bad people. They'd had an inordinate sway over her
life and now she was here, all alone.

As she lay on the examining room table of an abortion clinic, a
worker manipulated the transducer from an ultrasound machine
on her slightly protruding belly. The ultrasound confirmed what
her pregnancy test and instincts had told her. That which she
feared was now proven true. She was pregnant, and there in
the small room in the back of an abortion clinic, she was

immediately offered a chance to make yet another bad decision—did she want to terminate her pregnancy?

The technician was cool about the whole topic. She chose her words carefully to not engage Erin's heart any further than necessary in what was really a black and white question to many in the medical community: There was a fetus; was it wanted or was it not wanted?

Erin was confused and scared, but the truth is hard to ignore when you've been raised with it from childhood. She understood what that question really meant. To terminate a pregnancy, to eliminate what she saw there on the ultrasound machine, would be to kill her baby. She shook her head no, quietly got dressed, and slipped out of the clinic in tears. It had been several years of bad decisions that led her to this place and she was determined not to make another bad choice that she could never undo.

Later, she found herself sitting across a small table from a crisis pregnancy worker. The lady was kind as she listened to her story and offered solutions. They were not simple solutions. They involved sacrifice, whether it meant parenting this baby or making a plan for adoption. None of the solutions at hand were easy, but none of them led to death.

Erin decided that day to make a plan for her baby to be adopted. It was a step on a path far different from the path she had been on. Rather than overwhelming her with guilt and shame, this path led toward redemption.

For decades, the deck has been stacked against a woman choosing life for her baby. Society, financial pressures and Madison Avenue's portrayal of what a woman ought to look like and do have all conspired to make murder seem logical and childbirth seem like a fate worse than death.

With aggressive marketing by abortionists and promises of simple procedures, it is far easier for a pregnant young woman to end the life of her child than it is for her to carry it full term. With abortion comes what appears to be a quick resolution to what could be a life long problem. Abortion also allows a woman to hide her sexual activity. Ironically, many moms reason that by having an abortion, life goes on as normal. In reality, one life stops and another is never the same.

In dealing with the issue of unwanted pregnancy, the Church must come to terms with the fact that the situations at hand are far more complex than they appear at first glance.

Since 1973, we have focused most of our energy, our passion, our money and our efforts on saving babies. A baby saved was the ultimate goal—often the only goal—of the pro-life movement. They became the poster art, the rallying point, and often, the only thing we thought about when considering what it meant to be pro-life.

While there is a certain preeminence in saving the life of the innocent, we have failed to consider what choosing life and adoption means in the life of a mother. From an eternal perspective, there are at least two souls in this dramatic equation (three actually, although due to the nature of many unwanted pregnancies, the birth father's role is far less prominent than the birth mother's). While the church sees diapers and rattles, the whole story of a woman carrying her baby to term includes sickness, fatigue, financial strain, worry, and fear. Yet in the midst of this, many women do choose life and adoption, and in doing so discover the incredible power of redemption in making an adoption plan and placing the baby in a family who is willing and able to raise it.

When we refer to the redemptive power of adoption, we are not saying that the act in itself redeems the woman's soul. Those who find salvation do so by the grace of God and the blood of

Jesus. At the end of our lives we stand before God based on His mercy and our agreement with His nature and Word, yet none of us make that decision or find that grace in a vacuum. Our journey to faith and redemption is less of a straight line and more of a zig zag from experience to experience. Some of those experiences move us closer to grace while others can serve to pull us away. The sum of those experiences and our managing them is what places our heart in a position of receiving mercy from God. In light of that, adoption plays a remarkably redemptive role as one of those experiences that allows a young woman to draw closer to her heavenly Father.

Adoption is redemptive in the space it creates for grace.

By the time a woman finds herself at a crisis pregnancy clinic or on an abortionist's table, she is often at the end of herself. She has exhausted most means of support. She has come to terms with the fact that the birth father was interested in her body but not her heart. She is contemplating what life will look like, either with another mouth to feed or the heaviness that accompanies taking the life of one's own child. She looks forward with eyes cast down, spirit heavy, and much despair.

In His sovereignty, God can move how and upon whom He wishes, but often our own decisions make space for grace in our lives. By the leading of the Lord, we make what seem to be small, inconsequential, free will choices that accumulate to position our hearts, our lives, sometimes our very bodies in a place where we are more receptive to God. We choose to attend a church where we hear an influential sermon, we choose to befriend someone who eventually has great godly influence in our lives, or we choose to reach beyond ourselves to meet someone else's need and find the very presence of God there ministering to us. It's something akin to Sandra Bullock's character in the award winning movie, "The Blind Side". As her friends marvel at her family's adopting a teenage boy, they say, "You're changing that boy's life!" She quietly corrects them, "No. He's changing mine."

In making an adoption plan, a woman takes a very proactive role in the life of another human being. She is saying, "In spite of what this costs me, in spite of how people might react, I choose to give a good future to my baby." In making that choice comes a certain amount of breathing room, the realization of something having been done right for a change, that allows a woman to ponder the love of God as expressed by those around her. In speaking life over her baby, she positions her heart to hear the Father speak life over her. By simply regarding life as precious, she begins to ponder the worth of her own life. Could it be that she means as much to God as this baby means to her?

Adoption is redemptive in the role it allows the Church to play.

The Church was designed to be more than simply a legislative force for good in the world. It was intended to be a source for hope in hearts. As we've talked about earlier, the majority of the Church's voice regarding the unborn has revolved around one word: don't. Don't abort. Don't kill your baby. Don't act like this is so hard. You've made your mistake; don't make another. Don't, don't, don't.

While all those messages are essential and true, no one has ever found their way to hope by following a series of signs that say, "Don't". Every parent knows that children respond best to a combination of consequences and positive reinforcement. The consequences teach us what mistakes to avoid, but the positive reinforcement teaches us how to live right tomorrow.

When the Church steps into her role as a hope distribution point, she gains equity in people's lives. People may respect and obey a church that focuses on "don't", but they'll make life adjustments, daily decisions that effect eternity, wherever they find their hope. In making adoption a priority, the church projects a message of hope to a young woman who hasn't heard much about hope in a while.

Imagine the equity that a church would have if it were able to convince a woman that there was hope for her baby to be cared for in a way that she may not be prepared to provide, or hope that she can move toward her own goals of a job and a family of her own in due time.

In one sense, giving hope is as evangelistic as the four spiritual laws. It builds a path for a birth mom to walk and then commits to holding her hand. That path leads to far more than a resolution to her pregnancy. It leads to redemption.

Adoption is redemptive in the sense that good decisions lead to good decisions.

Have you ever watched a person make one bad choice after another? Just when you thought it couldn't get any worse, he found a way to compound his problems. He failed to maintain his car, so the engine blew up. Rather than fixing the car, he traded it and got almost nothing for the trade-in. He bought the new car at a high price and financed it at a high interest rate. By skipping a $30 oil change, he began a series of decisions that led to a $400 per month car payment.

Conversely, some people seem to have the golden touch. They make good choice after good choice, seeming to have everything going for them. Of course, everyone makes mistakes, and everyone hits a home run once in a while—but generally, people either make a lot of bad decisions or a lot of good decisions. That's because of what Robert Schuller called the Peak to Peak Principle.

The Peak to Peak principle works this way: we all go through mountains and valleys in life. Sometimes we're on top of the mountain of success, other times we're in the valley of failure.

The course corrections we make while in the valley are made without the benefit of the broad, mountaintop view. People making decisions on the heels of having made bad decisions are predisposed to make even more bad decisions. People making decisions after a series of successes have the distinct advantage of a healthy perspective.

Most birth moms come to the place of choosing between abortion, parenting or adoption after a series of deep valley choices. Like Erin from earlier in this chapter, they don't get to the clinic randomly. They find themselves there after making one bad choice after another. This is why so many choose to end their babies' lives—in light of the path they're on, it's the next step in the same direction.

There is something to be said about spiritual momentum, both upward and downward. The right choice of life leads to the right choice of Christ.

Adoption is redemptive in that iniquity and guilt are avoided.

Despite what a woman might feel regarding her pregnancy, her relationship with the baby's father, her family's reaction and what it all means for her immediate future, none of these is her biggest problem. There is something that looms far larger than any of these. With or without her acknowledgement of it, the biggest issue facing a birth mom is the issue of sin and guilt.

In most cases when a woman is pondering an abortion, there is already an overwhelming load of sin and guilt. Sex outside of marriage, rebellion, and all that goes with it converge in this one place and time and the simple answer provided to her by the abortion clinic, the one that seemingly makes it all go away, actually compounds the problem exponentially. What started as remorse for illicit sex leads to remorse for murder. One evil deed does not undo the other.

In making a choice for life, a woman avoids a lifetime of guilt. Without a doubt, there will be days when her heart aches for what might have been, but it will not ache with the guilt of having taken an innocent life. Making an adoption plan does not relieve guilt for actions past, but it certainly avoids an additional load of guilt that often proves to be more than a woman can bear.

Months after Erin walked out of the abortion clinic, she found herself in a hospital room. Sitting next to her bed was a social worker who had become her friend over the previous months. Down the hall, in another room, an adoptive mother was oohing and aahing over her new baby.

Erin was at peace. It wasn't an easy road, but it was the right road. If you ask anyone who's done the right and hard thing if they'd rather have done the wrong and easy thing, they'll tell you it's worth the struggle to do right.

There was a gentle knock at the door. As it opened, the woman who walked in looked strangely familiar. There had been so many faces through the room in the past 24 hours that at first, Erin couldn't place her. Then, in an instant, she remembered. This was the woman who had counseled her at the crisis pregnancy center. This was the warm face who spoke of hope after the abortion clinic had spoken of death. This was the lady who helped her make her first good choice in a long while.

After the visit, Erin lay there and pondered her situation. She had a long way to go, but she was moving on without the guilt she might have had, one good decision behind her and a lifetime of good decisions ahead of her. Christians that God had placed in her life had played the role of providing hope. There was a spot in her heart for God to work where she wasn't sure there was before. Her difficulties were not over but the scene had certainly shifted.

She was on redemption's path. Thanks to adoption, she was pointed in the right direction a little further down the road than she was before.

SIX

Divine Dreams

After a long day of work and responsibility, many people long for the moment our head hits the pillow. There, as we drift off to sleep, we not only recharge our physical bodies but our spirit is allowed a moment to rest. The relentless tide of life's pressure recedes for a moment. Our phone is not ringing. The TV is not on. Our email inbox does not command our attention. We are at rest.

In that moment that so many term as an escape, it is often that God speaks to us, whether we recognize it or not. The Bible is full of such stories.

Joseph infuriated his brothers when he shared his God-given dream of greatness. With much excitement, he tells them of the things he sees in his sleep. These dreams point to a day when he will rise above his brothers, but his brothers have another plan. They throw him in a well and later sell him to a band of traveling merchants. Eventually, he finds himself in the service of a pagan pharaoh, managing the resources of a nation and positioning himself to provide food for the very brothers who sold him into slavery. Walking out his God-given dream proved redemptive in every sense of the word.

God gave Daniel insight into the dreams of the king. Time and again the king called him in to his chambers to interpret dreams. This gift of interpretation elevated him to a place the upper echelon of Babylon envied, even though Daniel himself was only a slave boy. When God gives you insight into what He speaks into the spirits of men in the dark of the night, you find yourself in the most unusual places.

The prophet Joel promised dreams at the end of the age, and Peter referred to that promise in the book of Acts. While there are certainly times when a dream is merely the result of exhaustion, an over-active imagination or even too much pizza, there are also times when the Spirit of the Lord finds our hearts quieted in the midst of the night and speaks to our inner man. Those are the dreams that burn within us when the night is long over.

We had pondered adoption for many, many years, but the fuse of the rocket was lit with a dream. In 2001, we were church planting with a small group of young married couples on the north side of Cincinnati, Ohio. We had two sons, ages 8 and 4, and were early on in a pregnancy when Kelsey had a dream.

Years ago while I was pregnant with our third child, I had a dream. Now, I am a dreamer by nature. But this dream was different, you know the kind, when you wake up and feel as if you've just had a visitation. It was short, sweet, and to the point, but it had lasting impact.

In the dream, I was going to a prenatal appointment. My doctor met me at the door with a file folder in hand. He stopped me as I approached the door and, looking at the file, he said, "You will have a girl and you will call her Savannah Zoe."

Then I woke up. In real life, I was in my first trimester of pregnancy, so you can imagine the thoughts rolling through my

mind, that the Lord had possibly just shown me the gender of
the child I was carrying... and her name. I was ecstatic and
immediately began to search for the meanings of these beautiful
names God gave me in the dream.

I already knew the meaning of "Zoe," a Greek term meaning
"life" which seemed all too appropriate. What I learned about
the meaning of "Savannah" took the wind out of my sails:
"barren field" or "treeless plain."

What? Certainly this wasn't the Lord. We had prayed about
the name for this new baby and were quite sure that the name
would be a statement from God, a positive prophecy about our
child's life and future. But a "barren field"? I quickly shelved
the dream and labeled it "too much pizza before bedtime."
Still, something resounded in my heart that I was going to have
a baby girl.

Just days after this encounter with the Lord, a friend called who
I hadn't talked with in quite some time. She said she had taken
a nap that afternoon and had a dream about a little boy in
heaven. When she woke up, the Lord told her to call me because
the little boy in her dream was the baby that I had miscarried
months earlier.

This child was being held in heaven by my mother (who had
died the year before) and this was to be an encouragement to me
that God had not forgotten my pain. He was going to give me
the desire of my heart and bless me with children.

She also had a suggestion of a name for this new baby I was
pregnant with, "Zion." I asked her, "Is that for a boy or a
girl?" She said, "Either, but I believe this baby will be a boy
because the Lord says you need another boy right now." I didn't
tell her about the dream, and being convinced that I was going

to have a girl. I thanked her and we hung up.

"Bless her heart," I thought, "she is wrong, but that was nice of her to call."

A few weeks later we found out that the baby we were awaiting was a healthy baby boy. This all confirmed my thoughts that my first dream was not a spiritual one. However, I could not ignore the nudge deep inside that reminded me of the presence of God I sensed when I had the dream. Talking with God one day while driving down the highway, I asked Him, "Lord, what was that dream all about?"

What happened next is a moment that I will never forget. Sometimes God speaks in a still, small voice and other rare times for me it comes like a thunder. Immediately after I posed the question, there was a pounding in my spirit, and what seemed like a lightning bolt pulsed through my veins. I internally heard a thunderous voice call out, "Ezekiel 16." I burst into tears and nearly drove off the highway. The Lord had spoken and although I didn't understand completely, I was very aware that I had again been visited by His powerful Presence.

Over the coming days and weeks, I studied Ezekiel 16 with intensity. This chapter is the tender story of how the Lord "adopts" the people of Israel—an illegitimate people who are left as a baby to die in a barren field. The prophet tells how the Lord Himself came and covered this baby, taking it as His own, caring when no one else did and giving her a life and a future.

> *Ezekiel 16:4-6 (NLT)*
> *On the day you were born, no one cared about you. Your umbilical cord was not cut, and you were never washed, rubbed with salt, and wrapped in cloth. No one had the slightest interest in you; no one pitied you or cared for you.*

*On the day you were born, you were unwanted, dumped
in a field and left to die. But I came by and saw you there,
helplessly kicking about in your own blood. As you lay
there, I said, 'Live!'*

*The puzzle pieces were coming together from the dream:
perhaps the baby the doctor was talking about was this baby in
the Ezekiel story, "Life from a barren field". Still not understanding how this could be literal, I wrote it down in my dream
journal and kept it hidden in my heart, hoping the Lord would
give more revelation on the meaning in days to come.*

*In July 2001 the Lord blessed us with a son—whom we
named "Zion Isaiah". The friend who called me with the
name had passed away unexpectedly not long after we talked.
I know the Lord is into dreams and names... and He had
my attention.*

Dreams are sneaky. They can lie in wait and raise their heads in
the places and times that make the least sense. Then, when you
think you have figured out how they'll play out, they disappear
for a season. Often, later they spring up again, almost forgotten,
yet very much alive. Even though Kelsey initially thought the
first dream might have meant nothing, she continued to ponder
it in her heart like Mary when an angel visited her. Then, some
time later, another dream came to her.

*After the initial dream, we moved to a new city and were very
done with having babies. Adoption seemed like a dream of the
past and we were happily pursuing new avenues of life. Then
another dream came.*

*In the second dream, we were gathered with our small group
in a cozy home with a fireplace. It was winter outside, but*

warm in the house and we were all enjoying the fellowship of being together.

I went to the balcony of this home and stood looking out into a large field. It was dark outside and snow covered the ground. Suddenly, my eyes caught a movement in the snow. As I looked more intently into the darkness, I realized what I was seeing was a baby lying in the field.

I ran down the stairs and out the door into the field, desperate to find that baby. As I reached the child, I saw she had on a pink snowsuit and there was a discarded baby bottle on the ground beside her.

Instantly, I scooped up the crying bundle and held her close to my heart. A Hispanic woman appeared out of the darkness and she seemed angry. Instinctively, I knew her to be the baby's mother and that she was the one who had thrown the baby on the ground.

She grabbed the baby from my arms as I pleaded with her, "Please… if you give me the baby I will keep her and take care of her. I promise."

She handed her back to me and ran into the darkness, where she got into a car and sped away. I took the baby upstairs into the warm house and showed her to our friends. Several of them helped me look over the child to see if she was ok and we took her to a back room to clean her up and get her new clothing.

It was as if the Lord had given our community an invitation to receive the orphan.

Even with these two dreams and the realization of what they might mean, we could not have written a script that better intertwined it all. In October, 2006, God hit the "play button" on the prophetic story of our lives. Years of dreams and preparation began to work in sync.

> *On a Tuesday afternoon, I received a phone call from a social worker in Las Vegas. A baby girl had been born the day before. The social worker described her as "half African American, half Hispanic, with a gorgeous head of hair."*
>
> *My head spun as I sat down on the corner of our bed. I was almost afraid to get excited. Had my daughter been born halfway across the country? I knew it was customary for birth moms to choose from a number of prospective families. "How many portfolios are you presenting to the birthmother?" I asked.*
>
> *"Just yours. She's here in the hospital. Sir, if you want her, come and get her."*
>
> *Other than Kelsey saying "Yes" when I married her, I'm not sure when any other words have had such an emotional effect on me. It was as if I was getting thumped in the chest. "If you want her, come and get her."*

Adoption can be expensive and this particular adoption was going to be at the higher end of the spectrum. The social worker talked to me about fees and I quickly knew we were about $7000 and airfare short of what we would need—and we'd need it in days.

Within minutes, God provided the plane tickets with frequent flyer points from a friend, so we booked a flight for the next day. The next eighteen hours were spent scurrying around, gathering last minute paperwork, running to the police station for fingerprinting, packing a quick suitcase, and probably sleeping a few hours, although I don't remember that part at all. The next morning before we left for the airport, I typed out a fast email to friends and others who had been following our adoption process. It told of our situation and bluntly said, "We need cash... can you help?"

An hour or so later, waiting to board our flight to Las Vegas, I opened my laptop for a last minute peek at email. A new message appeared on my screen with news that made me shout for joy. "We were watching a documentary last night on the potential for revival in Las Vegas," the note said, "and we want to invest in Las Vegas by wiring you $7000." With that, the money for our adoption was completely provided.

I'd been in the Nevada desert a number of times before, but neither of us had ever been to Las Vegas. We'd never had a desire to go. In fact, the slight experience we'd had with Las Vegas was not a good one.

Some years before, Kelsey's parents both fell ill with cancer. Tragically, they died within 100 days of one another. Due to some bad financial decisions and their expensive illnesses, they both died nearly penniless. Her father left her a box of engineering books and some change on top of his dresser. Her mother died with a hundred dollars in her bank account. Although they were reconciling at the time of their death, they had spent the last season of their lives separated. As a result, they had lost their family home and all the contents. In that home was everything that was left of Kelsey's childhood; toys, photos, and mementos of earlier times. Kelsey lost her parents, and in sense, she lost her past. There was nothing left in the way of an inheritance.

As the plane began to descend, we were watching out the window as the desert gave way to subdivisions and golf courses. Somewhere over the campus of the University of Nevada - Las Vegas, Kelsey and I experienced one of those unusual visitations of the Lord. We both heard Him in a silent inner voice as He spoke the same words to both of us: "I have sent you to this city with real money to buy back an inheritance for Jesus." We wept to realize the brilliant design of God's redemptive plan in our lives and the life of this little baby.

As we raced through the clamor of the Las Vegas airport on our way to the rental car counter, I received a phone call from Lou Engle, founder of TheCall. We had been in conversation about our giving direction to a series of arena-sized gatherings for fasting and prayer across the nation. He had just been given a check to cover the rental of the Titan Stadium in Nashville for TheCall to be held the next July. At the time, my mind was anywhere but my duties with TheCall, but the phone call from Lou in Las Vegas would later prove to be part of God's grand drama.

In our rented car, we made our way through afternoon traffic to the University Medical Center, with one brief stop to buy a video camera. We laugh about it now. We had raised three little boys without so much as thinking about a video camera, but this was our little girl! It seemed everything was different.

Walking into the hospital, we found a nurses' station and asked to see a baby by the last name we had been given. The nurse on duty gave us a blank stare. "Who?" she asked.

I repeated the name. She looked at her computer screen. She checked a file. She glanced at a clipboard. She consulted with another nurse who gave her the same blank stare.

"I'm sorry, we don't have a baby by that name," she said.

A million thoughts raced through our minds. Was this a joke? A cruel hoax? Had the baby been removed from the hospital? I couldn't believe we had come all this way for nothing.

A half second later, a third nurse chimed in. "That baby is downstairs in neonatal," she said.

It was as if the upside down earth had righted itself. I could breath again. We had to restrain ourselves from running down the stairs to neonatal... after all, our girl was there!

The nurses in the neonatal nursery were expecting us. We were whisked through a waiting area and into the nursery itself. Two rows of bassinets sat in the center of a large room, head to head. We followed a nurse down the row, looking at each puff of hair protruding from the bundle of blankets, wondering "Is this one ours?"

Near the end of the line, the nurse turned on her heels and warmly told us, "This one... she is yours." Truer words have never been spoken. She picked up the baby and handed her to Kelsey, then directed us to a small room off the nursery.

"Go in here," she said. "You can have some privacy." With that, she shut the door and we were alone in the quiet with our little girl. We pulled the blanket back from her face and stared. Kelsey gently sat in an easy chair and, as she gazed at the face of her new little girl, began to weep. In that moment, every dollar, every form filled out, every phone call... it was all worth it.

After a short time with our little bundle of joy, we left to go to our hotel for some rest. We would return the next morning to meet with the social worker.

We had been referred to this adoption agency by a friend in the adoption business and had been told, "Be aware. It's not a Christian agency, and it is a business." The next morning, again with Zoe in our arms, we were excited to hear our social worker tell us, "Everything looks good on your paperwork, but if you're praying people, it never hurts to pray a little as it goes through."

We chuckled. We assured her we were praying people. One thing led to another, and she began to tell us the story of her pastor and their church. They wanted to build a prayer tower on a nearby mountain that would overlook the city of Las Vegas. Reaching across Zoe, who lay sleeping between us, she pointed to the mountain and said, "A few months ago, Lou Engle prophesied that there would be a house of prayer on that mountain that would contend with every false ideology in Las Vegas... have you guys ever heard of Lou Engle?"

Kelsey and I stared at each other. The lengths to which God would go to orchestrate the rescue of this little girl were astounding us. He had knit together a cast of characters around prayer, breathed a little prophetic wind on it and sat back to watch the fun.

A few days later, someone emailed us a note about the meaning of Las Vegas' name. It seems the area was named in 1829, when Spanish explorers noticed a small oasis in the desert and named it "Las Vegas"—meaning "The Meadow." It was another one of God's poetic touches. We were so happy to bring Savannah Zoe—this little girl, rescued from a meadow or open field like the baby in the book of Ezekiel—back home with us.

Even then, it wasn't over. Almost one year to the day of leaving Las Vegas with Zoe, we were back in the city. This time, rather than a hospital, we stood on a large stage erected in the University of Nevada - Las Vegas basketball field house. We stood near our new friends, Paul and Denise Goulet, the social worker's pastors, and with Lou and Therese Engle, giving leadership to TheCall Las Vegas as 8,000 people gathered to pray and fast for a move of God in their city. I had been privileged to spend much of the previous six months networking within the city and doing the behind the scenes production for this massive gathering.

The $7,000 gift sown into the hope for revival in Las Vegas the year before was still paying dividends. The baby rescued in the desert was there in our arms. Our full inheritance, bought with real money and a touch of the prophetic, is still yet to be fully realized but it started like that for so many others with adoption.

Many of you have dreams. They've come in the middle of the night, or even as you sat looking out a window. They're a glorious mix of the voice of God and the desires of your heart. Even those desires are things that God gave you.

You may find yourself wondering how these things will ever come to pass. The goals seem too lofty or the situation too hopeless. The details are too scattered. You could never make it happen. You can dream the dreams, but just barely. You certainly can't bring them into the now.

We couldn't either. Never in a thousand years could we have orchestrated all it took to bring Zoe home. We never had enough money, enough connections, or even enough imagination to weave it all together. Even in the months after it happened, we were discovering how the hand of God had been at work.

Fortunately, the dreams we all dream are not our dreams alone. He is allowing them to rest in your heart fully knowing that He has a perfect plan to bring them to fruition. Don't shrink back from those dreams. They are the stuff of God's handiwork yet to be done.

SEVEN

The Rewiring of the American Dream

As we mentioned earlier, we adopted our first daughter, Zoe, from Las Vegas, Nevada. The very mention of the city's name causes a reaction from many people. They roll their eyes or shake their heads, knowing that for most people, just below the glitter line, Las Vegas is a city of broken dreams. That made it all the more poignant when, walking in to the nursery to see our little girl, Las Vegas was a city of dreams realized. Finding new life there has, for me, always served as a not-so-subtle symbol of what God wants to do in the hearts of residents of this city in the desert.

That said, the reputation the city has is not undeserved. The better known side of Las Vegas remains intact. Whether standing on the wide, well manicured streets of the western suburbs or walking down the Las Vegas Boulevard, what everyone calls "The Strip" in the neon faux-daylight that shines 24/7, you realize that this is a city of winners and losers, and while the winners control the spotlight, the losers inherit what remains. Once, cutting through a casino to get out of a hotel, my son Grayson—then 9—took one glance at the vacant faces of the slot machine players and asked with incredulity, "Dad... are these people having fun?" For the moment, yes. But moments do not last.

If you drive north of the Strip in Las Vegas, past the casinos, wedding chapels and glitz, you'll be within blocks of the hospital where we first held Zoe. You'll also be at a place marked on the tourist maps as The Neon Museum, although none of the locals call it that. To them, it's simply called, "The Boneyard."

The Boneyard is the final place of rest for all the old signs that used to beckon people to the gambling establishments of The Strip. The dusty back lot off Freemont Street is a veritable neon sign graveyard. Get out of your car to walk The Boneyard and you'll find the former marquees of Caesar's Palace, The Silver Slipper, The Golden Nugget and other Las Vegas icons. Some sit at awkward angles with lights broken out, in such states of disrepair that it's difficult to know exactly what they were inviting you to originally. Others were better cared for and placed here by people who love the artistic element of neon and pizzazz. They look as they did in their heyday, with one exception: their bulbs that once glowed brightly no longer shine. The signs are there, but there's no power attached.

These neon behemoths, both gaudy and attractive, were the drawing cards of days gone by. At the time of their implementation, the signs were so brilliant that thousands flocked across the desert from the East or over the Sierra Nevadas from the West, ecstatic when they got their first glimpse of neon on the desert horizon. Most believed that under those signs they would find wealth and the good life they longed for. These were the signs that drew them to Las Vegas. They promised a short cut to riches, and fed the lie that with those riches would come happiness.

In the intervening years, the signs have lost their luster. The marquees that once towered over the traffic a half mile to the South now lay abandoned and forgotten in the dirt. Bulbs were broken. Wires were disconnected. All that glittered was not gold.

In fact, it wasn't even a sustainable facade. They've been replaced by new attractions up and down The Strip. You may come to Vegas looking for the neon of The Golden Nugget, but once you get there, newer signs catch your eye and you end up at the Bellagio. Even if you are a hard core fan of Caesar's Palace, you may only stop briefly to pay homage, and then you move on to brighter and bigger things, completely missing the irony that those brighter and bigger things will find their way to The Boneyard one day as well. In fact, even as you look to the bright lights of the south and determine that is where you want to go, men in board rooms on the top floors of the casinos are plotting their next big extravaganza, because they know what you are about to learn: once you arrive, it doesn't take long for all of it to appear hollow.

The Failing American Dream

There are few metaphors available to us that better illustrate the futility of the American Dream. Our country, founded on a yearning for spiritual freedom, was simultaneously financed by money hungry profiteers. As our history played itself out, we cultivated an intellectual ascent to freedom in the cities of the North while holding others captive in the South to keep our national economic machine running. The banks in the North counted on the profits from the South. Whether endorsing slavery or not, most Americans benefited in some way from the system.

Things have changed, but not that much. We may have moved beyond wholesale slavery, but most Americans still buy the lie that bettering oneself is usually just a matter of economics. We still think that if we can just cash in, life will be so much better. We justify this narrow perspective of success with a grandiose label: The American Dream.

In his 80s hit, "Allentown", Billy Joel sang "everyone had a pretty good shot to get at least as far as his old man got..." We have been groomed to believe that our birthright as Americans includes a ticket to a bigger house, more finances and more influence, and that to do anything other than reach for those goals is to somehow fall behind the pack. After all, isn't that what it's all about: more money, more fame, more ease and more accomplishment?

In a word, no.

The American Dream will one day prove to have made us all terribly short sighted, and will be the initiator of the Great American Headache. Even now, we see clear indicators in the aftermath of the housing market implosion. We are beginning to admit that the expectation of each generation to prosper more than the previous generation simply cannot endure. Those opulent, over-mortgaged homes, that so many thought were a must-have, will be found in the cultural Boneyard, a symbol of days and entitlements gone by. In time, our children will look at them as relics and shake their heads, wondering how we fell for it. Unfortunately, many of them will set their own sights on goals as banal as ours were, because they will still believe that success means getting all you can.

One of the toxic underpinnings of the American Dream is the notion that this life is all we get, that all we will experience, influence or enjoy takes place during the tiny blip of seven or eight decades. If that is true, it makes sense to grab for all we can. If The Dream is true, then our prime earning years are best spent on ourselves, because no one but us is thinking about us. Any satisfaction we might know will be the satisfaction we create for ourselves. We would be justified in living large, spending big, taking what we can get and leaving none for the others. That is, if it's true. Most of us have a love-hate relationship with The Dream, betting everything on the chance that it holds water, but sorely afraid that it won't.

Deep in our hearts, we have our doubts. It's almost as if we anticipate disappointment. We reach for the brass ring but we suspect it's plastic. After our spending, after our consumption, after all the Me we can stand, we suspect that there is more to life than making it big. If our suspicions are right, then surely there is an alternative set of values that we can leverage for a greater experience, larger influence, and more enjoyment in this life and beyond. If it's not just about us, then who is it about, and how do we best invest this limited quantity that we call life?

The Las Vegas hospital where we met Zoe for the first time is just blocks from The Boneyard, literally just down the street. In that gray concrete bunker of a public hospital, in the shadow of the longest running get rich quick schemes in our nation, I started thinking my first thoughts about what it really meant to be rich, and what it meant to trade personal renown for maximum influence.

I'm embarrassed to admit that I didn't think this way earlier in life, particularly because the Bible explains it clearly. Psalm 127:4 likens children to arrows in the hand of a warrior. Even though I already had three sons, this was the beginning of a serious reevaluation for me as I considered what it meant to be successful.

It's unclear when the bow and arrow entered human warfare, but we do know this: it was a battleground changer. Until then, violence was limited to man on man; you could only hit what you could reach. Out of reach meant out of danger. The bow and arrow must have come as a real shock to the first soldier who found the enemy raining pain down from the sky on his men.

With the advent of the bow and arrow, a man could be dangerous in places far beyond his ability to travel. Though he could never reach his enemy on foot, he could strike him down from a distance. It extended the range of his dominance far beyond his own normal capabilities. He began to have tremendous power in places that he could not get to. Using the bow and arrow, His range of effectiveness exceeded his natural ability.

When the Lord places children in families, He is placing arrows in quivers. The battle between good and evil is radically altered. No longer is the parent's influence limited to their own life span. True mothers and fathers are able, through their influence on their children, to make a difference decades beyond their own death. If that child raises godly children, the impact goes even deeper and broader.

The American Dream, which continually prioritizes the individual, ceases in its appeal at the moment of death. It is far exceeded by the Kingdom Dream, which can shape both the now and the later. In comparison with the American Dream, this influential Kingdom Dream of impact that transcends death seems far more productive and rewarding. Who would willingly choose to limit themselves to only their generation?

Our world is full of scattered arrows.

Imagine for a moment you are on a battlefield. The ground around you is littered with arrows. You may have none in your quiver, or you may have just a few. In fact, you may even have more than the average, but these arrows are at your feet. What do you do?

Of course, in the heat of battle, you scoop up the arrows that you can. Why? Because you know these arrows, properly released, will go much farther than you could go alone. Those who gather the arrows and win the battles eventually gain the authority to propagate their values and ideologies over the conquered land. An arrow in your quiver is the primary way that you'll extend your influence beyond yourself, and any arrow that you can get your hands on has double value. You are the one who sends it into the future, and it's an arrow your enemy does not have control over.

In having children, naturally born or adopted, you extend your influence beyond the seventy-some years that most people spend on this earth. If people are limiting their influence only to their own lifetime, one hundred years from now, most people's lives will be unrepresented. It is for this kind of person that grave markers are so important, because without chiseling his name in stone, it would cease to be spoken of once he passed away.

The same person who instead intentionally influences children with his own values will find those values represented perpetually and far more broadly than he may have represented them during his own life. Simply put, if you're convinced of something and want to convince the world, convince your children and wait. They will scatter like the wind and take your ideas with them. With your message tattooed on their heart, they will go further and faster than you ever could.

The Muslim faith understands this concept of children as arrows far better than the Western version of the Christian faith does. While the West wrings its hands over the idea of overpopulation—which for most people, is really more of a concern about money than space—the Muslim world concerns itself with representation leading to domination. We're concerned if we'll have enough resources; they're concerned with developing widespread influence.

Demographers will tell you that the average American Christian family has slightly over one child. This is generally not because of health reasons or inability to conceive. The lure of convenience and a perceived demand for a certain standard of living causes people to stop having children to better be able to afford the finer things. In many cases, the idea of another child is forced out and replaced by the idea of a newer car or an extra week of vacation.

Few will come right out and say they don't want children,

but fewer still will pay the price of having them. Consciously or unconsciously, people are most often choosing between children and ease.

This mentality seems uniquely tied to our Western mindset where we like our houses large, our families small, and our lives unencumbered with the million things that children demand. Those families who choose to upsize, to forgo the second car or the yearly vacation for the sake of another life, appear to most of their neighbors as a bit of an oddity.

Worldwide, Muslim families are generally larger. Even in the US, where Muslim people appreciate the finer things in life as well, the average American Muslim family has just under five children. While the Irish and German and Latino immigrant families may have come to the US with large families, usually the legacy of many children comes to a stop by the third or fourth generation. Not so with Muslims. Three and four generations into the American experience, Muslim families do not bow to the cultural norms of family size. They place the value of a larger family ahead of the value of comfort. They grow large families and continue to change the face of our subdivisions, our schools and our courts.

While this is interesting in what it might mean over the course of a decade, the real genius of it doesn't display itself for another forty or fifty years. Consider this: not allowing for spouses, three generations of Christians will mean a net gain of two people. Three generations of Muslims, however, will mean thirty.

The Christians must proselytize just to keep their population level. Even if the Muslims are only 50 percent effective in influencing their children for Islam, they are still stacking the deck for a comparatively huge Muslim population in just a few short years. Who is actively preparing to influence this country three decades from now, followers of Allah or followers of Jesus?

Muslims are not the only segment of the population that

are looking to children as social influencers. In recent years, the gay and lesbian community has embraced adoption in record numbers.

Most states already allow homosexuals to adopt, either by fiat or by simply ignoring the issue. Many states that don't are moving in that direction. Most of those that don't allow homosexual couples to adopt will allow homosexual individuals to do so, thereby allowing for children to go into the homes of homosexual couples who are not allowed by law to marry in that state anyway. In other words, gay adoption of some sort happens in almost every state, and it's growing fast.

When we adopted our twins, we were surprised to be asked to sign a statement declaring that we were not gay. Weeks after we adopted our twins, the state of Florida changed its law to allow for gay adoption. Had we not moved quickly, the twins would have entered foster care for a period, and then been available to this new pool of adopting couples.

Why the surge in gay adoption? Simply put, they are looking for two things: to legitimize their relationships and to propagate their lifestyle. Even in the areas of the country that are friendly to the idea of gay marriage, the gay "family" is defined as two individuals of the same sex. Adoption is the only way that they will extend their "family" beyond two adults, and so they do what they need to do to replicate adherents and cultivate a larger population, sympathetic to the belief that this is just an alternative lifestyle rather than a biological dead end. It's sadly ironic that they have latched on to this value of snatching up the scattered arrows that the church is willing to step over.

Homosexuals are not alone in their sudden interest in children. There is a growing, global criminal element that seeks to leverage possession of children into a sizable fortune. While the homosexuals are looking for legitimacy, the child traffickers are in it for the money. Any place you find a large number of children who are not well supervised and otherwise cared for, you will find people trying to lure them into captivity, where they will be whisked away from all that is familiar and repeatedly assaulted until they believe the lie that sexual perversion is what they were made for.

Abortion advocates have long made the argument that the babies that are presently being aborted are simply babies that are unwanted. They rationalize the murder of those in the womb by saying that if these children are allowed to live, they will not come into the world wanted and loved. Planned Parenthood's slogan is, "Every Child a Wanted Child." They finance their murderous campaigns on the idea that they are doing society a favor in ridding it of what it will not embrace. If we can prove them wrong by holding to the value that every child is wanted, we can break their grip on a generation of unborn children.

Their argument will not stand. It's already crumbling. In our lifetime, both sides of the spiritual divide are coming to a point of agreement: children are, in fact, wanted. However, the bitter truth is that they are wanted for vastly different purposes. It is a clear marker of the end of the age when the homosexuals, the child traffickers and the prayer movement are all shouting the same thing, "Give us the children!"

The Christian mandate for adoption is bigger than just a positive alternative to abortion. The church's call to adopt is a call to embrace and influence the future. In the US alone, the lives of 4,500 per day are up for grabs to be influenced for good or evil. Worldwide, you could multiply that number many, many times. Those are simply the numbers of those who are presently being killed in the womb. Factor in those who are alive but not cared for, and you can see how we are facing an army of neglected children, millions strong; an army that will rise to arms one day soon. All that remains to be decided is who will train them for battle and on which side they will serve.

The nudge you feel in your heart to adopt is not a romantic notion. It's not about filling your minivan or providing you with a child you did not conceive. It is about fulfilling the prophecy of Malachi by turning your heart towards children before the great and terrible day of the Lord. Even as we fight for their lives now, the question looms over the debate: who will they fight for in the future? That largely depends on who reaches out for them in their day of need.

One of the great failures of the church today is dreaming too small. We have fallen for the lie that the great American Dream, the bigger house, the fancier car, the 401k, are the best we can hope to have and to pass on to our children. The Kingdom Dream of the Lord is that we would provide our children something far more extravagant than a manicured lawn and a mortgage, but access to a King that will reign forever, and a role as coheir to Jesus in His Kingdom.

The adoption movement is not merely anti-abortion. It is pro-life, pro-future, and pro-Coming of the King. We are not in this arena to rescue children only in the present, but to give them access to the Throne of God for all eternity. That is a dream worth living for.

EIGHT

Myths about Adoption

Our season in Washington, DC during most of 2005 was an incredibly formative time for us. As we stood in front of the Supreme Court, God shared a prophetic strategy that would be a tangible way for families across the nation to get involved and put feet to their prayers: to adopt and care for the very ones they were praying for.

It seemed overwhelming at first. We knew little about adoption and what little we did know was inaccurate. Answering the call to adopt felt a little like jumping off a cliff. Even saying it out loud seemed like a holy commitment, one that could not be rescinded. It's wisdom to think before you jump... but sometimes, it's also wisdom to go ahead and jump. We jumped in with both feet and soon found that adoption is filled with miraculous activity, mundane paperwork, and myths. We were astounded to watch the myths begin to shatter as we learned more.

The myths surrounding adoption are developed in a number of ways. Most often, someone hears of someone else's unusual experience and retells the story as if it's the norm. Other myths are propagated by profiteers in the adoption industry. There are thousands of godly people working to help adoptive families, but as in any other area where there is much emotion and finances at stake (medical care, insurance, funeral homes) there are also people who are in the business to make money. Even so, rarely do these people flat-out lie, but they often exclude a portion of the truth to make their help seem more valuable than it really is.

Other times, myths are simply propagated by ignorance. People cannot be blamed for what they do not know, but what they don't know often holds them back.

Our experience in adoption exposed a number of beliefs that are wrong or misleading. These myths need to be countered with the truth at every opportunity.

Myth #1 There are no babies to adopt in the U.S.

If the topic of adoption is raised in a group, invariably someone will say, "We want to adopt internationally because we want an infant, and there are no infants available in the United States." Understand that we wholeheartedly support international adoption. The United States offers opportunity like no other country on earth and any child who can be rescued from an orphanage in Ethiopia, Ukraine, or a host of other nations, will be blessed as will the family who welcomes them. That said, international adoption should be considered, but not simply as an easy alternative to domestic adoption. It is not intrinsically easy. International adoption requires the same amount of paperwork as a domestic adoption does, and often more, along with the additional difficulty of navigating cultural and language barriers.

The idea that there are no babies in the US often comes from the story of a cousin or distant friend who had to wait an extended time to adopt a baby. There are multiple reasons why an adoption may take an inordinate time or perhaps never happen at all. The agency may be less proactive in connecting with birth mothers than other agencies. The country that they are adopting from may suddenly change the requirements. The family may not be willing to travel out of their region to adopt.

Think of how many people search for the right house for a year or more in a city that may have hundreds or even thousands of homes for sale. All the same reasoning applies. Perhaps the baby destined for them is not ready, or perhaps they're simply not realistic in what they're expecting. The result is the search takes longer, but it's not for a lack of babies.

The same is true for adoption. Some couples have idealistic expectations for adoption. A woman looking to adopt approached us and said "I have two blonde haired, blue eyed girls... if you could find me one like them, that would be great." She's probably still waiting. Likewise, other people want 100 percent assurance that the child they will adopt will be perfectly healthy in every way. Never mind that no biological parents are offered that option. For some reason, when people go to adopt, they can get remarkably picky and unreasonable. That said, the vast majority of babies that are adopted are completely healthy, and they're all adorable.

Every day in America, babies are born that go straight into state foster care because the mother is not prepared to parent or did not think ahead to make an adoption plan for her child. In our second adoption, the hospital had called the state twice asking them to send someone to receive the twin girls that were taking space in the nursery because no plan was in place. In our first adoption, the social worker called us because we were the only family they could find on short notice who was willing to accept a biracial child.

There are babies available in America; and there are growing children desperately in need of homes as well. Every state in America has a foster care system. In most cases, there is even financial assistance available for families willing to accept children from that system. We recently heard of a family of five children that were all perfectly healthy. Their mother had passed away and their father was unable to care for them. Does the church in America have the capacity to embrace these children and keep the family together?

Whatever is keeping you from adopting, don't let it be the myth that there are no children available, because there are, and there will be more when the grip of abortion is released from this nation.

Myth #2 It's too risky

While the myth of unavailable babies is blatantly false, the myth that it's too risky is more one of perspective. When people ask me if it's too risky, I always ask, "As compared to what?" We have an irrational fear of some risks and perhaps an unhealthy acceptance of others.

People jaywalk across on a regular basis, yet will hide under the covers in a thunderstorm, even though last year 42,000 people were killed in car accidents while only 90 were killed by lightening. We willingly accept some risks because the perceived pay off is worth it.

We often hear, "We saw this thing on television where a family adopted a child and…" followed by a story of a birth mother changing her mind, a legal battle, an illness, or some other one-off example. We're quick to remind people that Hollywood makes movies out of exceptions to the rule. Marketers will tell you that, "Family adopts a baby, everything goes smoothly" is not a plot of a best selling movie, yet it is by far a more common occurrence. A well counseled and cared for birth mother rarely changes her mind. A legal adoption is designed to be lock-tight in court. And as for illness, do not children born from your own flesh and blood also get ill? Has no one ever suffered the loss of a biological child?

We would not say that adoption is risk free. We would say

that risk is inherent in anything of value in life. We all love with our hearts held open. Legal adoption with the right counsel minimizes the risk of almost everything people fear, and for the things that it is not able to minimize, we have the grace of God. If we didn't believe in the ability to minimize risk and the power of God to move, none of us would ever purchase a home, ride in a car, or even cross the road. Some risks are worth the payoff. The life of a child is at the top of that list.

Myth #3 Adoption takes too long

This is a cousin to the "no babies available" myth, based on some people's one-off stories and sometimes, unrealistic expectations. The discussion about this myth usually goes like this:

"We'd like to adopt, but have heard it could take a whole year..."

We ask "Do you have biological children?"

Often the couple will say, "Yes, we do."

"How long were you married before you decided to have children?"

"We were married two years, then we decided to have a baby. We were pregnant six months later."

"So when was the baby born?" we ask.

At this point, they stare at us and wonder if we understand much about biology. "The baby was born nine months later, of course!"

"Okay, so from the time you decided to have a baby until you gave birth to that baby was fifteen months, and yet adopting a year from now seems like it's too long to wait? It's faster than getting pregnant and having your child biologically!"

While there are babies available, adoption is a process. Interested couples must fill out paperwork, attend interviews, get medical exams and take fingerprints. It may seem like a lot of work for nothing, but you're asking professionals and the government to place a child in your home. It really is for the children, remember?

The long, drawn out adoption is the exception, particularly if you've found a reputable agency or consultant to work with. Don't think of it as going to Costco to pick up a child. A baby is being born and there is a process both biologically and administratively that must happen. Adoption does not take an inordinate amount of time, and the amount that it does take is easily worth the wait.

That said, there are times when adoption moves incredibly quickly. Our first adoption took four months from the time we made the first phone call until Zoe was in our arms. Recently, our agency helped match a home-study ready family to a newborn in a matter of weeks. Those are best case scenarios, but if you're open to travel and adopting children of other races, it can happen very, very quickly.

Myth #4 Adoption is too expensive

Those who investigate adoption are often stunned at the amount of money that the process can cost. We nearly choked when we were first looking at agency web sites and clicked on the button marked FEES. We felt dizzy for a moment looking at their estimated expenses of $25,000 plus medical and legal fees. It was definitely out of our comfort zone, given that we had a family budget that rarely allowed us to purchase a full tank of gas.

It might have been a stumbling block for us were it not for two things: we are incredibly stubborn and a little naive. We knew that God had called us to this and we believed that He took care of His bills.

We were troubled that a woman could abort a child for $400 but somehow it cost $25,000 to place that baby in a loving family. We believed this inequity was an affront to God, but we didn't let it discourage us. We felt the Lord asking, "Will you put what little money you have where your prayers are? Will you believe Me to bring in the money as you lay your lives down for the sake of children?"

Randy spoke with a professional who advised him of the fees associated with adopting. Gently, that professional asked, "Have you set money aside for this expense?"

"No," Randy answered. "Does that scare you?"

The person on the other end of the phone said, "No... not at all." We later found out that she really was concerned that we were diving in with no funds! Sometimes it's a gift to be unaware that others think you're a little crazy.

The zealous heart of a man or woman on a mission can pave the way for the impossible. We went on to challenge our friends to sow into a vision bigger than just our own family—a vision of an adoption movement spreading across the nation in answer to the cries of the unborn. We challenged people with the idea that giving to help one family adopt was the beginning of a million adoptions, that there was coming a movement of families that would willingly forego the price of a movie ticket, signing up for another car payment or even their daily $4 latte because lives were more important than comfort.

The adoption industry is expensive. That offends some people to the point of refusing to be involved, insisting, "I don't want to contribute to a corrupt system, so I'm going to boycott it until there is a better way." They seem to assume that the babies being born today, tomorrow and in coming months will somehow wait until the perfect system emerges that allows them to adopt for the price of a cheeseburger. They will still be waiting in ten years, a decade older, with the cries of thousands of children ringing in their ears.

Chapter 10 will deal with how we can work with and change the system, but in the meantime, private and state-run adoption agencies are placing babies in homes across the nation. Many are non-Christian homes. Many are the homes of those in the gay and lesbian community. Why not your house? Why not now, whatever the cost? Sometimes, as a forerunner you have to play the system to gain the authority to beat the system. Later we will talk more about this idea and what can be done to lower the costs nationwide, but initially, the adoption movement will have to pay the price of admission to gain the right to be heard.

In the early 1800s, Elihu Embree was a wealthy slave owner with a large estate in East Tennessee. He became personally convicted on the issue of slavery and started the first abolitionist newspaper in the US. His paper, *The Emancipator*, boasted a circulation as large or larger than any paper in a two state area. His voice rang out loud and long before many people were talking about ending slavery, and his work remained influential throughout both the North and the South for decades after his passing.

Becoming a revolutionary in the war over slaves, he realized he had to free his own slaves. He carried within him conflicting values—one for freedom, the other for the value of his estate. Knowing that he needed to put his own fortune on the line, at great personal expense, he freed the slaves he bought along with those he received from his father-in-law when he married his wife.

Embree knew that the revolution would be worth the cost, that one day, blacks would be born free, but until then, people like himself would need to pay a high price. In paying that price, he bought freedom for men that day, and paved the way for a day when they would be born free. He gave up his fortune and his future for the freedom of a generation.

Those involved in the birth of a revolutionary movement always have to bear a higher cost than those who come behind and reap the benefits. It's the cost of a revolution. We're not the only ones involved in this revolution. There are thousands of people like us, and perhaps you are one of them. You certainly have an invitation.

We understand the outrage. We agree that paying $20,000–$30,000 to adopt a child is a travesty, but don't let the price of a used car be enough to deter you from changing someone's eternity. The next chapter will address some ways to raise the funds to finance this revolution.

Myth #5 We already have enough kids

There is an acceptable number of children to have in our culture, and when you cross that line, society lets you know. As nearly as I can determine, the number allowed is three. Even though the average American family has less than two children, there is grace for three. With three boys, we received approving nods. People smiled and made comments about the old TV show "My Three Sons". We were a bit of a novelty, but certainly not an affront to anyone's sensibilities.

With the addition of the fourth we received a few second looks, but even then, the three older were boys and the fourth was a girl, so people understood our excesses. They assumed we wanted a girl so badly that we were willing to go through the trouble of having four children.

Of course, then we added numbers five, six and seven in rapid succession. We became members of the Fifteen Passenger Van Tribe. At one point, after gathering the stares walking through a store, Randy threatened to have matching t-shirts printed for each of us proclaiming, "Welcome to the Freak Show."

A family of three children was normal. A family of four children was quaint. A family of seven children was more than society could fathom or keep quiet about. We receive a steady stream of advice and strangers "counting noses" as we walk by. Sometimes, we get a thumbs up. More often, people shake their heads and mutter things like, "Don't you know what causes that?"

We've taken to cheerily answering, "Paperwork!"

The truth is, it's only our culture telling us that we have enough kids. For most of human history, families were much larger than they are now. Of course, when we moved from an agrarian culture to an industrial one and then on to a digital world, the need for children to work alongside us dissolved. Our houses have grown larger, our disposable income has increased, our leisure hours have extended and our families have gotten smaller. This is not because we can't handle as many children but because we don't have the use for them.

What if the highest purpose of a child is to learn and be discipled in the ways of the Lord? What if we start thinking about the upper limit of family size not in terms of comfort and more in terms of influence? We're not saying that every family must have a family as large as ours, but that if a couple chooses to have a larger family, they make a certain trade off in immediate convenience that pays eternal dividends.

With seven children, there are things we will not get to do. There are probably ministry trips or family vacations we won't be able to take. There are undoubtably books that won't be written on schedule. Immediate productivity will suffer, but if we parent well, even if our children only have two children each, in two generations we will have produced twenty-one families with our values. Those families will scatter across the globe and take with them the lessons we have instilled in them. Suddenly, all of our temporal sacrifice seems well worth it.

Have you ever prayed the prayer of Jabez found in the Bible?

1 Chronicles 4:10
And Jabez called on the God of Israel saying, "Oh, that You would bless me indeed, and enlarge my territory, that Your hand would be with me, and that You would keep me from evil, that I may not cause pain!" So God granted him what he requested.

That's a dangerous prayer. Expanded territory means expanded responsibility. Even so, expanded responsibility means expanded influence. God may very well answer this prayer in a way that stretches both your borders and your heart!

Perhaps you're looking at your family right now—you feel cramped in a small house, working off a small budget. What you may not realize is that your house would feel like a royal palace to many children languishing in foster care systems. Your attention could make all the difference in the world to them. What feels like a little bit of nothing is more than they'll ever have without you.

Additionally, most of what your children learn will not be by what we tell them, but by what they see us doing. In opening your home to more children, you will drive a message deep into the hearts of your existing children: because God is a God of plenty, there will always be room for one more at our table.

Adoption radically expands the hearts of the children you already have. In most cases, kids are more excited about adding to the family than parents are. They know that it's going to mean cramped quarters, smaller allowances, and needing Mom or Dad to multitask a bit to hear everyone, but intuitively, they know it's worth it. Don't let society predetermine your family size. Ask the Lord what His capacity is and then lean on Him.

NINE

Generational Links

—∞∞∞—

Fresh out of Bible college with big dreams of changing the world, we got married and moved to rural Kansas where we had accepted the position of youth pastors at a tiny church in a small town. There had been no writing on the wall that this was the perfect place to start our new life, but the job was available and we were under the impression that youth pastoring was the route to go when aspiring to full-time ministry.

Admittedly, we didn't have a passion for the area or even for young people. We just wanted to do our time and get to where we were going. Perhaps that was why we were successful at taking the youth group from five members to three!

It didn't take a genius to see that our heart really wasn't in youth ministry other than to get to what we would have called "real ministry". Somehow, in our zeal to take the world by storm for Jesus, we had forgotten it's not all about us, and if we wanted to influence the nation, we needed to influence the future leaders that would be representing righteousness and justice in the years to come. Like it or not, at the end of the day, we are all youth pastors because our lives are much less about us and our destiny and much more about securing an inheritance for Jesus when He returns. To pastor young people is to pastor the future.

When we talk about our destiny, we're usually talking about promotion. From our perspective, destiny is seemingly linked to promoting us out of the mundane and into something greater, more glamorous, with a higher position and greater visibility. What if we've got that all wrong? What if our destiny is truly to serve the younger generation with faithfulness while staying on the bottom rung of the ladder? What if we are called to be the floor which the children walk on to get to the next level? This kind of thinking doesn't fill conference venues, but perhaps it should. Sacrificing for the next generation is one of the keys to opening the door for the glory of God to fill the earth.

God has a plan for each of us. He wants us all to enter a realm of greatness and glory, but in our western culture, it has become all too easy to think only of ourselves as we climb the ladder of success. Society tells us it's a dog eat dog world, that you have to fight for your rights and you can be anything you want to be. While it can inspire us to work harder, this is the mindset that will leave our children with a big mess to clean up and nothing to glean after we are gone.

Aspiring to have influence means that we have to consider the effect our actions have on the generations to come, not just on our own lives. What legacy will we leave behind? As they gather around our casket once our spirit has left our cold, dead frame, what will they talk about? Will the sum of our accomplishments end with our final breath, or will what we've lived for continue to grow and develop because we left it to others?

Believers have a universal command to pass on wholehearted devotion to the Lord to the next generation. This is not a new command; it's as old as time itself. The mandate is not trendy; it's difficult, time consuming and overwhelmingly unpopular in a microwave world that cannot pay attention long enough to see the cause and effect. Nevertheless, it is a command so important for the human race to understand that God took Moses to a mountain, manifest His presence with fire and wrote it on his heart so that he could carry it to the nation.

> *Deuteronomy 6:4,5*
> *Hear, O Israel: The LORD our God, the LORD is one! You*
> *shall love the LORD your God with all your heart with all your*
> *soul, and with all your strength.*

Jesus calls this the "greatest commandment"—greater than the Ten Commandments which were penned with the very finger of the Almighty—because love trumps all. In Matthew 22:37, Jesus basically says, "Hey guys, if you get anything I am saying, get this!" We are to love the Lord wholeheartedly and teach our children to do the same.

The sixth chapter of Deuteronomy is not only a command to wholehearted devotion, but it's a strategy for passing it on to the next generation. God knew that one generation does not automatically pick up on the cues of the generations that have come before, so he initiates a plan to keep His message moving through the generations of history.

> *Deuteronomy 6:6-9*
> *And these words which I command you shall be in your heart.*
> *You shall teach them diligently to your children, and shall*
> *talk of them when you sit in your house, and when you walk*
> *up by the way, when you lie down, and when you rise up.*
> *You shall bind them as a sign over your hand, and they shall*
> *be as frontlets between your eyes. You shall write them on the*
> *doorposts of your house and on your gates.*

The master plan isn't hard to figure out. He simply says, "Tell the story!" It's that easy. Talk about what He has done and what

He is going to do. Make it a part of your "to do list," the core of your life plan—tell the children His story so that they will know Him and love Him. At the end of the day, along with "Did I remember to pay the mortgage" and "Did I take out the trash?" we have to ask ourselves "Did I tell the story?" The master plan is that children would hear His story from their moms and dads, resulting in God being not only the God of their fathers, but the God of their own hearts.

Our oldest son, Jackson, had an epiphany the year he graduated high school. He has known the Lord as long as he can remember, having asked Jesus into his heart at a children's church meeting when he was four. He was mostly an obedient, compliant child, never rebelling outwardly and almost always striving to please.

Jackson was twelve during our adventure with the Justice House of Prayer in Washington, DC. He found himself daily with a group of teens and twenties, standing on the steps of the Supreme Court, fervently praying for the ending of abortion, and spending many evenings rumbling in prayer with them in a little prayer room near the Capitol. This had a remarkable effect on him.

On his thirteen birthday, he decided he couldn't celebrate because, in his words, "One third of my friends have been aborted." He reasoned that there should be thousands more celebrating their thirteenth birthdays that year. Deciding to forego a traditional birthday party with cake, he called a fast and asked friends to join him in the prayer room to pray that abortion would end. Hundreds from around the world emailed him to tell them they were participating with him.

Over the years we have seen him grow in the grace and favor of the Lord. Even so, as much as he had experienced in his youth, as graduation approached there was an angst in his heart over where he was headed in life. He certainly had options—there were many open doors for him. Unfortunately, the decision regarding what direction to take was not coming easily.

Finally, after receiving a word from a wise mentor and then choosing to fast and pray, he made the decision to enter an internship where he would give himself to a year of pursuing the Lord in a focused way. After being immersed in a childhood of prayer and us teaching him about the Lord, he said on his internship application, "Before, I engaged because of my parents. This time, I am going to find the Lord for myself."

This was a profound statement, and it made us so very thankful for what the Lord was doing in his life. The stories we had told and retold, the conversations over dinner, the decisions we had made as a family, they had led this young man to pursue God for himself. Although at times we felt so weak in our understanding of how to walk it out, the Deuteronomy 6 strategy worked in Jackson's life to cultivate his own hunger for God.

Habakkuk 3:2 (NIV)
Lord, I have heard of your fame;
I stand in awe of your deeds, O Lord.
Renew them in our day,
in our time make them known

As parents, it is the cry of our hearts that the stories we tell won't end up on the same shelf as the fairy tale books. Just like the prophet Habakkuk prayed, we love the drama of the stories of old, but we want our children to have their own story!

How many times have you read a book to your kids only for them to go and act it out? Our son Zion would love to hear the tales of David slaying Goliath, or David fighting the Philistines. For a long time, his favorite toy was a wooden shield and sword. Armed with that sword and shield, he'd head out to the back yard to bring to life all the stories he had heard. He slew many a rosebush in those days. The stories were inspiring, but he wanted his own victories.

There is an innate desire for us to live our own adventure in the Lord. How better to lay the foundation for a life story in God than to fuel that desire with the greatest drama of all time? God knew that little boys would be drawn by the tales of giants falling and armies being slain. He was aware how little girls would react to the story of a peasant becoming a princess or being the bride in the most glorious wedding of all time. The stories of old, when told with passion, can fan the flame to pursue their own stories, authored by the God of the universe. What more could we ask for?

When our boys were toddlers, Randy began telling them the many stories from the book of Daniel. We decided to pray a prophetic prayer over them from that book at bedtime. Each night, they would hear, "You are a mighty man and you will do great exploits for God." At some point, one of us had the grand idea that not only should we pray this over them, but we should teach them to speak it for themselves, declaring the promise of God for who they would become. For years, each night they would speak those words, "I am a mighty man and I do great exploits for God!".

One evening, when Grayson was only four, he fell asleep on the couch before his dad came home from teaching. As Randy carried him back to his bed, he whispered in Grayson's little ear, "What are you going to be, son?" Without waking up, that little four year old muttered "I am a mighty man… and I do great exploits for God." The stories of their lives were being ingrained in their spirits.

Another time, as we were tucking the boys in bed, Grayson looked up with tears in his eyes and said, "Momma, I want to have a garage sale and take all the money and buy popsicles for poor people." He was disturbed to think that he would have so much and there were people in our city with so little. He went

*on to insist that we pray for the poor of our city and make a
plan for serving them before he rested. It was obvious that the
Lord was touching his heart so we encouraged him, "Grayson,
you are hearing from the Lord. This is a great exploit! See, your
prayer is working! You are a mighty man!"*

*Through his tears, he smiled and said, "Yeah, it's working! It's
not working on Jackson yet, but it's working on me!" We had a
good laugh about the sibling rivalry, but rejoiced that the life of
a man of God had sparked the desire for Grayson to have his
own God-story to tell. Since that day, he's had many adventures. Truly, God's storytelling strategy works!*

For God's people, the command of wholeheartedness came with
a promise: a homeland, a place in which to settle and belong.

Deuteronomy 6:18
*And you shall do what is right and good in the sight of the
LORD, that it may be well with you, and that you may go in
and possess the good land of which the LORD swore to your
fathers.*

Within us all is a longing for a home and a place to belong.
Throughout the eighties, each week the TV show Cheers began
with a theme song heralding the bar as a place where "everybody
knows your name." America gathered around its TV sets, determined that if they couldn't find a place to belong, they would
watch a fictional place where people had found one. If you didn't
have a home, then the local bar would do.

There is a resurgence of "community living" in our day. Developers are building "co-housing" subdivisions in cities across
the US to meet peoples' desire to live in closer proximity and
tighter community. As we dive into the mandate of God to love
Him with all our heart, mind, soul and strength, we find a promise of that place we long for and the confidence that it's ours

now and always. When we pass the torch of this promise onto the next generation, we have become part of the great chain of history, faithfully stewarding the word of God and becoming a prophetic link, joining the ancient heroes of the faith and the young generation of today.

Do you remember making long paper chains from construction paper in grade school? Children cut strips from the paper, loop them around one another, and glue the ends. This is done over and over until the chain spills off their desk and onto the floor. They take them home for their gracious mothers to hang their art on the Christmas tree to be displayed for all to see. Unfortunately, the chains are always delicate, and the glue never seems to hold well. Inevitably one of the loops will come apart and break the chain, making the whole thing fall to the ground. One weak link in the paper chain reduces a work of art to a heap on the floor. Even if all the other links are solid, that one weak link ruins the effect.

Most often we think of humanity as a mob of people, but in the case of a family, a paper chain is probably a more accurate picture. In the chain of history, God doesn't want a weak generational link. Without each link passing on the story, the chain doesn't continue. He wants each generation to develop a strong bond to the next, passing down the great stories and commandments, in order that His glory would cover the earth as the waters cover the sea. You're not just a lone individual, you're a link in the chain that stretches back to Adam and forward to the end of the age.

If a person is looking for maximum influence over time, they would be wise to adjust their perspective from one of amassing a fortune or merely spending fifty years working hard solely for fifteen or twenty years of ease. The question should not be "How much can I accomplish for myself while I walk the earth," but rather "How many lives can I link to? How many paper chains can I extend from my vantage point. How many can I tell the message in such a way that they would want to live it out on their own?"

When we think of our lives as just that, a link in time, with its purpose to glorify God and pass on a message to those who come after us, it can change our whole paradigm of living. It influences how we spend our money, our time and our talents. We end up doing things that may seem out of the ordinary to someone who is setting themselves up for a life of ease, but are perfectly rational to the person asking, "How can I extend the story of God to the most people?"

Marcus and Rachel are a young couple in our community. We've known them for years, having met Marcus shortly after they were married. In their late twenties, they have four beautiful young children. Their lives are busy with ministry opportunities and family obligations. No one would think twice if they hunkered down to take care of life for a while.

Recently, Marcus saw Randy driving in our big fifteen passenger van and waved him down. "Randy!" Marcus said. "I just bought a van like this!"

Randy laughed at him. As our family grew, we held out as long as we could before driving the big white van that needs to be parked on the far corner of the parking lot. The idea that a young couple in their twenties would go out of their way to drive one was humorous to him.

"Really?" Randy asked Marcus. "You did?"

"Yes! We're leaving for Ethiopia in a few weeks to bring back twin girls and we need the space to haul them!" Marcus was elated about his van, not because it was a cool ride, but because of what it represented. He was choosing to drive a big van because it allowed him and Rachel an opportunity to be a link in God's story to these two little girls.

Adoption is not a spur of the moment decision. Neither is it a haphazard, emotional commitment that a person makes because they want to do something good for someone else. It is a conscious decision to limit one's own options, pleasures and even potential for the sake of extending the story of God to children who, without a link to you, may never discover their link to God.

Regrettably, marketing has made adoption seem more like a warm, fuzzy adventure than warfare, but in reality, warfare is exactly what it is. It is stepping up to serve as a link in the chain, refusing to allow a child to grow up disconnected from their heavenly Father. This approach to adoption will bring the rage of Satan against you to discourage you, to tell you it's not worth it, you can't afford it and you probably won't be good at it anyway. That is the way of warfare; it's what Satan has always tried to do. If you're committing to adoption you need to tune a deaf ear to him and remind yourself, "I'm a link in this little one's chain. I'm not the whole story, but I'm the one entrusted with delivering the story right now."

For the first year or two, Zoe wasn't a very good sleeper. She was a happy baby but most nights she'd be up for an hour, maybe two, crying in the night. There was nothing that we could do to comfort her, so we'd take turns walking the floor with her, hoping she'd settle down before the rest of the house woke up.

One night, after an hour and a half of back and forth, she would still not be quieted. Randy was holding her as he tried unsuccessfully to get back to sleep. The next morning, over a badly needed cup of coffee, he told me that as he was walking with her and praying for her, he heard the Lord ask, "Would you adopt her again?"

The question startled him. "Of course," he prayed "of course I'd adopt her again."

The Lord spoke clearly in Randy's spirit. "That's what adoption is. You adopt her every day. Every day you decide to love her. You decide to make her yours. You decide to show her how she is Mine. You make a choice to adopt her every day."

It was then that Randy began to understand how important each day was in building that link between the God of our fathers and the hearts of our children. Each day had to be lived intentionally. Nothing could be taken for granted. We adopt them every day and pray that we instill in them the sense of who God is and what they mean to Him.

There is a battle raging for the hearts and souls of children. The enemy knows that if he can capture their hearts he will have delivered a true blow to the Kingdom. He also knows that if those hearts come to know their Heavenly Father, there is nothing that will stop them. The most practical way for those children to come into their destiny is for them to come into a family first.

Will you be a link in the generational chain that will know the Lord?

TEN

The Call to Action

W e are meant to be people of action. From the beginning, in the garden, we partnered with God. God purposely left some things undone to allow man an opportunity to be a part of his great plan. "Here," God said, "name the animals." Was it because God was exhausted and needed some rest? No, it was because He wanted partnership from the very beginning.

God could choose to bring immediate justice to all the orphaned, abandoned and unborn. Instead, He offers us the dignity of being a part of the solution.

In hearing about the opportunity of adoption, people often wonder, "How can I get involved? What can I do?" It's partially because their emotions are moved, but it's also because it's the divine plan for them to play a part. They were meant to be people of action.

If an adoption revolution is going to take place, it will require participation both by individuals and churches to bring as many children to Christian homes as possible. There will need to be intentional steps taken involving time and budgets. Without these efforts, the revolution is no more than talk.

Individual Participation

Adopt a Child

On an individual level, the first practical thing to do would be to get a home study done and prepare to adopt. There are almost as many ways to do this as their are children available.

You could go through your own state's foster-to-adopt program. This is often an inexpensive way to go, albeit with a few extra steps in the way of classes and accountability. Each state varies widely in their skill at administrating their foster to adopt program, so ask around until you find a family who has gone this route before. Ask them about the good, the bad and the ugly. You may find a system difficult to work with or you might find it very supportive and helpful.

Another route would be through an adoption agency that will work with you to match you with a child. These agencies often work across multiple states to help you find a match that is right for your family. A good agency will do all it can to care for the birth mother before, during and after pregnancy as well as protect the legal interests of the adoptive family.

Contribute Financially

It may be that your family is not called to adopt, but that doesn't mean you're not called to be involved in the spirit of adoption. There are a myriad of things you can do to promote the cause and help other families adopt. One such thing would be to contribute financially to the adoption expenses that a family is incurring. Before an agency even considers a family eligible to be matched with a baby, that family will have spent at least $1500-2000 in home study fees, doctors visits, FBI fingerprints. During our first adoption, the realization hit us that a large part of the adoption process was signing our names on checks, repeatedly. Consider what you might be able to do financially or professionally to ease the burden. Recently, we had a doctor tell us, "When you know of families who need home study physicals in my city, send them to me. I can do those for free." In another city, an attorney told us, "I would happily adjust my fee to match the family's income." These are excellent ways of helping trim the costs of adoption for a family that is signing up to care for a child for life.

Serving an Adoptive Family

Another way to get involved is to help practically with the transition of a new baby entering the home. When a baby comes to a family by biological means, there are nine months of planning, praying, and pondering what it will be like. Sometimes adoptions happen so quickly that people don't have the luxury of getting things ready.

> *When we adopted our twins only 30 hours elapsed from the time we learned of their existence until we carried them out of a hospital 1,000 miles away. We literally raced to the airport while a friend followed our instructions to get us on the next plane to get us as near as we could that night.*

> *The next day, we went to the store to buy two car seats, a box of diapers, some formula, bottles and a few clothes. As Kelsey sat in the lobby with the twins, I was racing to unbox and install car seats in the hospital parking lot.*

> *Strangers walked by and shook their head as if to say, "Why didn't that man prepare?" The truth is I couldn't have prepared; I didn't know until the day before that we were having a baby, much less twins! I didn't bother telling them that part of the story as it would have only led to more incredulous questioning.*

While not everyone's adoption process is as fast as ours, truthfully, adoption is often quite the adjustment to the adoptive family. Years ago, family would always come around and assist a couple when a baby was born. In our world, family is often an airplane ride away. God needs to raise up uncles, aunts, grandpas and grandmas who can help.

God has blessed our family with a number of others who come alongside to help us make life work. There are several twenty-something girls who have become extended members of our family by giving us a few hours each week. There is another couple whose children are nearly grown. They are not personally called to adopt, but they understand their call to the adoption movement, and they regularly pitch in to help us with practical deeds of service.

Two years ago, we purchased an old home that had been uninhabited for nearly three years. The growth of bushes had gotten completely out of hand. One Saturday, a crew of nearly thirty people, many who only knew us because of our adoptions, descended on our yard to cut brush and pile it. While they may have held clippers that day instead of a baby, they were a vital part of the adoption movement because their work allowed us to do what we're called to do.

Look for families in your community or church who are adopting and pitch in. Speaking from experience, you can help the most if you're specific about your offer, follow through, and be willing to take instruction. For example, if you say, "I'd like to help you guys. You know, whatever you need. Tell me. I'll help," I can almost guarantee you aren't going to get a call. On the other hand, if you say, "I am coming Thursday afternoon to mow your yard," you're going to be a hero. Unless, of course, it's a Thursday in January… but you get the idea. Specific offers of help by people who show up and follow through are like gold to a new adoptive family.

Church Involvement

Everyone can get involved as individuals, but there are some things better done corporately. There are also ways that your church can get behind adoption and allow many people to participate who otherwise might feel like spectators of the adoption movement.

Think Missionally

For a church to begin thinking intentionally about getting involved in adoption, it first needs to talk about adoption in a missional way. Pastors need to understand that it's okay to recognize an adoption in the church in a different way than a husband and wife who are having their own child through biological means.

James 1:27 talks specifically about widows and orphans. Romans 8 talks about the spirit of adoption. These are very real, biblical truths that are best illustrated when a Christian family takes a child into their home and gives that child a name. A pastor who learns to use that as a teaching moment will both inspire others to adopt and drive home a point about our own spiritual journey by giving the biblical concept of adoption a face and a name.

Strategically Fund Adoption

In days gone by, a church commonly stayed out of the realm of an individual's money. Perhaps because of that approach, debt is rampant in the church and many pastors are finding that they spend a significant amount of time counseling people with financial problems or addressing the issue of money from the pulpit. Many churches are now getting involved in the personal finances of their parishioners. One of the fastest growing church programs in America for the past several years has been Dave Ramsey's Financial Peace University, a thirteen week class that teaches people how to proactively manage their finances in a way that honors God.

With this melding of our church and personal finances, church leaders have a newly rediscovered responsibility to talk about good investments and placing our money where our values are. This goes beyond boycotting businesses who are an affront to our Christian values. This means investing our finances in places that further the Kingdom. A church that understands adoption will be a church that makes adoption doable for its church family.

Some churches have started adoption funds by taking a series of special offerings to build up a nest egg. These funds are available in small grants for adoptive families in their church, or as no-interest loans to help pay adoption expenses. One such group who administrates a no-interest loan fund said that even in a down economy, their default rate had been zero for many years. The fund just keeps replenishing itself. An individual who may have given $100 or $1000 years ago has been able to watch that gift invested over and over again as it's repaid and then passed along to the next adoptive family. The church nursery was filling up with babies whose families had tapped in to that fund.

Launch an Adoption Agency

When we launched The Zoe Foundation, our initial vision revolved around helping finance adoptions. Since then, we've branched off into education, networking, and a hundred other things that help people adopt. We've continued to give small grants and coach others on how to raise the funds to pay adoption fees that often cost up to $30,000. Eventually, we began to wonder how practical it was to expect to launch an adoption revolution by giving people a few thousand dollars on a $30,000 bill. Then, by the grace of God, we stumbled into an opportunity that has been a true game changer. Yes, we could contribute a few thousand dollars to a ridiculously large expense, but what if we could somehow get that expense down as low as possible before a grant was even needed. What if we could *lower* the bill?

In January of 2009, we heard about an adoption agency that was up for sale. We began to consider buying the agency as a laboratory to see where the real expense was. There is rarely a shortage of ideas around our house, so it was a topic of discussion for a while. We have a small number of people in our life whose primary purpose is to keep us on track. I went to each of these people individually and described the opportunity, expecting each of them to tell me, "Run away from this opportunity. You're plenty busy already and you don't know anything about doing adoptions!" Incredibly, all four told me, "You have to do this," and the fourth individual offered to pay for the agency if I'd step up to the challenge.

I was right—I didn't know what I was getting into, but they were right too! Sometimes you learn the most by doing, so we decided to do adoptions until we understood how to do adoptions affordably.

What we learned was fascinating. First, we learned adoption is more complex that it initially appears. There are reams of laws and regulations, boards that interpret those laws and regulations, vast procedural difference from state to state, and national, non-governmental agencies who have the authority to make sure you do it right. Contrasting all those rules and regulations, you have the dramatic world of birth mothers who are laying down everything to bring life into this world, and adoptive parents who are making room in their hearts and homes with anticipation of a baby to come.

We quickly fiddled with the economic model to dramatically decrease expenses and then passed those savings directly on to the adoptive families. The agency we purchased was built on being profitable charging $20,000 in adoption fees. We found that with strategic savings, we could get that price down to $7,000. We also discovered that most churches are perfectly poised to do the same thing for their congregations.

One of the greatest expenses in an agency is salaries. In our case, the Executive Director's salary was significant. It wasn't ridiculously high, but when Randy became the Executive Director, he did so without taking a salary. That money came off the top of the adoption fees. In truth, being the Executive Director of a small agency is not necessarily a full-time job. In annual budgeting, it would serve a church well to ask a staff pastor to take this on as one third of his portfolio. The church pays a full salary for the pastoral duties, knowing that a portion of that staffer's time will go toward directing the agency.

Of course, an Executive Director alone cannot run an agency. There is need for social workers, administrative help, people to coordinate birth mother care, and a host of other things. We remember making our very first hire, an amazing social worker who instantly understood that this was not a normal adoption agency. Perhaps it was our approach that clued her in. Randy said "We want to change how adoption is financed and make it doable for families, so I'm inviting you to work hard for about half of what you might make somewhere else. You will never get rich here, but you will shake the profit-driven segment of the industry to its core."

With tears in her eyes, she agreed. Her drive to make a difference far outweighed her salary demands. It was in that moment that I learned you can pay people with things other than money. Everyone needs to pay their bills, but you can actually reward people with a role in the revolution that means more to them than any dollar amount ever will.

Later, the same speech gained the agency a Compliance Director, expertly skilled in interpreting the law and collaborating with state agencies, and a Family Coordinator who serves our adoptive families like they're her own. These are two professionals that I could never pay what they are worth, but when God saw what we were getting into, He knew we needed good help. He has these sorts of people hidden away in the cracks and the crags for you, but they'll only surface for a challenge that matches their skills and drive to make a difference.

Structured as a non-profit, the agency can also make use of volunteers for many roles. They need to have background checks like they would if they worked at any other agency, but they're allowed to volunteer their time. All the money you might have paid them can come straight off the top of the bill.

Another expense is real estate: an office, office equipment, etc. While churches are getting more creative about use of their space, most churches are still entirely unused six days a week. With a little juggling, they could carve out an office for an agency somewhere on the premises and save rent and utilities. By allowing the agency use of office equipment such as furniture and technology, you can save thousands of dollars. Again, this allows you to set lower fees for the families in your church community.

Meanwhile, as we were setting up the agency, The Zoe Foundation was continuing to raise finances to help people pay the bills. The result was our very first adoption some months ago. The adoptive family received a grant that lowered the already low $7,000 bill to $4,000 plus medical and legal costs. By attacking the financial barrier from both sides, we have made adoption doable for those who set their hearts to do it.

There were expenses with opening the agency, because some things cannot be done for free. For a season we rented office space. Our work required things, and even though the few salaries we paid were small, they added up. We looked at these start up costs as an investment in our agency's first adoption. It wasn't money up in smoke; it was money that would pay huge dividends.

We'd guess that we spent about $20,000 before we started collecting the fees that made the agency self sufficient with its meager budget in place. That sounds like a lot of money, but think about it this way: what if, by spending $20,000, your church could allow you to purchase a $35,000 car for $7,000? You would save $28,000, because they spent $20,000. And the next family saved $28,0000, and the next family after that. If only four families took advantage of this great deal, it would mean that the community got a 500% return on the initial $20,000 investment. Years down the road, when your church nursery is full of adopted children and you're still doing more adoptions, your investment has grown exponentially.

Now imagine for a moment that the savings were not on a car but for a human being. It's for the privilege of partnering with Jesus to give Him an inheritance. It's for placing an innocent child in the house of the Lord to be discipled and have his or her life trajectory focused on the knowledge of God. For a mediocre investment of time and effort, the church is unusually positioned to eternally change the lives of countless individuals.

It is not practical or wise to place the calling to adopt on every family in the church, but there certainly are families within your faith community who already bear that yoke. Additionally, the call to care for orphans truly does rest on the entire community. What better way to walk out that calling than to make it doable for everyone who feels led to do so?

ELEVEN

The Charge

W illiam walked home from his job one dark night and nearly tripped over a drunk in the gutter. The man was dirty, smelly, and mumbling incoherently. Within steps of his quiet house, his wife, and a warm bowl of soup, William was faced with a question:

Is this okay with me?

He could easily have stepped over the drunk and ducked into his own home, safe and secure. He worked hard, made a good wage, gave his portion on Sundays and kept out of trouble the rest of the week. No one was looking to him to fix this problem, but the question haunted him.

Is this okay with me?

Slowly he turned back toward the man, helped him up from the grime, and brought him into his home. He shared his soup. He gave him a bath, and later a bed. As the sun rose the next morning, over a hot cup of tea, William shared the love of Jesus with this man.

That experience changed the trajectory of William's life. He was shocked to find injustice right outside his doorstep. He was also shocked to discover the answer to the problem might lie in opening the door to his own home.

Not many years later, William Booth's organization, The Salvation Army, was feeding and clothing the homeless and hurting around the world. He wrote a bold plan for dealing with England's poor entitled, "The Way Forward." It changed the way a nation thought about meeting people's basic needs. His accomplishments were epic in proportion, but they began with a simple question.

Is this okay with me?

That's the question we have to answer regarding the large number of aborted children in America.

Is this okay with me?

More than 4,500 children a day torn from their mother's wombs in a painful death.

Is this okay with me?

Many children who do escape abortion end up in a foster care system that is often a farm team for the prison system and prostitution rings.

Is this okay with me?

If we move quickly, we can still duck into the safety of our own homes. We can gather with our family around the pot of soup on the table and if we keep our conversations animated, we can produce enough noise to drown out the cry of the orphan.

But some of you aren't okay with that. The soup in your own

bowl is unsatisfying knowing that, just outside the door, there are children who need good homes.

This is your call to action. This is your cue to move. If you've been waiting like David for the wind in the tops of the mulberry trees, the wind is blowing right now. It's time for action. Ask God what it means for you to be involved in caring for orphans, and then listen.

If He tells you to adopt, make the phone call to start a home study today.

If He tells you to give, find an adoptive family to help today.

If He gives you a vision for an adoption ministry, talk to your pastor today.

Whatever you do, don't let the sun go down without taking some sort of action. Start the ball rolling. Make your move. William Booth's revolution began the day he decided that he couldn't allow things to continue as they were.

With the sense of urgency that Booth felt that day standing over a man in the gutter, may an adoption revolution begin in your heart that sweeps around the world until there is no memory of a time when children were called unwanted.

The Zoe Foundation exists to further the cause of adoption as a positive alternative to abortion in America. It endeavors to do this in multiple ways:

- Helping fund the adoption of children into pre-screened families living out a lifestyle of prayer and fasting.

- Providing for quality care for mothers who are choosing to offer their babies for adoption rather than aborting them, along with follow-up care after the child is born.

- Educating the church about the redemptive power of adoption, the effect it can have on their own congregation, the difference it will make in eternity, as well as the practical steps to adoption.

- Assembling a national database of thousands of state approved, home-study ready Christian families who have said "yes, I can and will adopt a child", and providing access to that list to those who are considering placing a child up for adoption.

- Assembling a national database of healthcare and legal professionals who will assist in a limited number of adoptions on a pro bono basis each year.

www.thezoefoundation.com

Made in the USA
Charleston, SC
09 November 2012